Scribal Skips

1300 Words That Fell Out of the Bible

Wayne A. Mitchell

Copyright © 2017 Wayne A. Mitchell.

All rights reserved. No part of this book may be reproduced, stored, or transmitted by any means—whether auditory, graphic, mechanical, or electronic—without written permission of both publisher and author, except in the case of brief excerpts used in critical articles and reviews. Unauthorized reproduction of any part of this work is illegal and is punishable by law.

Scripture taken from New Heart English Bible by Wayne A. Mitchell. Public domain.

ISBN: 978-1-4834-6187-8 (sc)
ISBN: 978-1-4834-6186-1 (e)

Because of the dynamic nature of the Internet, any web addresses or links contained in this book may have changed since publication and may no longer be valid. The views expressed in this work are solely those of the author and do not necessarily reflect the views of the publisher, and the publisher hereby disclaims any responsibility for them.

Codex Sinaiticus image courtesy of Center for the Study of New Testament Manuscripts (CSNTM).

Lulu Publishing Services rev. date: 4/25/2017

Contents

Abbreviations vii

Acknowledgments xiii

Introduction 1

Haplography List: Old Testament 6

Haplography List: New Testament 59

Conclusion 95

Appendix 101

Abbreviations

A 02	Alexandrinus. c. 450 AD
ac	Akhmimic Coptic. 4th
Acac	patristic: Acacius Caesariensis. 366 AD
Ad	patristic: Adamantius. c. 300 AD
aeth	Ethiopian version. c. 500 AD
Aleph 01	Sinaiticus. 330-360 AD
Ambr	patristic: Ambrose. 397 AD
And	patristic: Andrew of Caesarea. 614 AD
Apo	patristic: Apollinaris of Laodicea. c. 390 AD
Apr	patristic: Apringius. c. 551 AD
Aquila	Aquila of Sinope. c. 130 AD
arm	Armenian version. 5th
Ast	patristic: Asterius, Sophist. aft. 341 AD
Ath	patristic: Athanasius of Alexandria. 373 AD
Aug	patristic: Augustine. 430 AD
B 03	Vaticanus. c. 300-325 AD
Bas	patristic: Basil of Caesarea. 379 AD
Bea	patristic: Beatus of Liebana. 786 AD
bo	Bohairic Coptic version. 4th/9th
Byz	Byzantine Majority text
C 04	Ephraemi. 5th
Cass	patristic: Cassiodorus. 580 AD
Chr	patristic: Chrysostum, John. 407 AD
Cl	patristic: Clement of Alexandria. 215 AD
Cyp	patristic: Cyprian of Carthage. 258 AD
Cyr	patristic: Cyril of Alexandria. 444 AD

CyrJ	patristic: Cyril of Jerusalem. 386 AD
D^{ea} 05	Bezae. 5th. Gospels, Acts
D^p 06	Claromontanus. 6th. Pauline epistles
Delta 037	Sangallensis. 9th
Diatess	Diatessaron of Tatian. c. 175 AD
Did	patristic: Didymus of Alexandria. 398 AD
DSS	Dead Sea Scrolls
E^e 07	Basilensis. 8th. Gospels
E^a 08	Laudianus. 6th. Acts
Epiph	patristic: Epiphanius of Constantia. 403 AD
Eus	patristic: Eusebius of Caesarea. 339 AD
Eva	patristic: Evagrius of Pontus. 399 AD
F^e 09	Boreelianus. 9th. Gospels
F^p 10	Augiensis. 9th. Pauline epistles
f1	Family 1 manuscripts. 10th
f13	Family 13 manuscripts. 10th
G^e 011	Seidelianus I. 9th. Gospels
G^p 012	Boernerianus. 9th. Pauline epistles
Gamma 036	Tischendorfianus IV. 10th
geo	Georgian version. 5th
GNT	Greek New Testament
goth	Gothic version. 5th/6th
GrNy	patristic: Gregory of Nyssa. 394 AD
H^e 013	Seidelianus II. 9th
(H)	retroversion to Hebrew
Hes	patristic: Hesychius of Jerusalem. 451 AD
Hier	patristic: Jerome (Hieronymus). 420 AD
Hil	patristic: Hilary of Poitiers. 367 AD
Hipp	patristic: Hippolytus of Rome. 235 AD
I 016	Freerianus. 5th
Ir	patristic: Irenaeus of Lyons. 202 AD
Is	patristic: Isidore of Pelusium. 435 AD
JohnD	patristic: John of Damascus. 749 AD
Ju	patristic: Justin (Martyr). 165 AD
JuCas	patristic: Julius Cassianus. 170 AD
Juv	patristic: Juvencus. 330 AD

K^e 017	Cyprius. 9th. Gospels
K^{ap} 018	Mosquensis. 9th. Acts, Paul, General Epistles
L^e 019	Regius. 8th. Gospels
L^{ap} 020	Angelicus. 9th. Acts, Paul
Lambda 039	Tischendorfianus III. 9th
lat	Old Latin version NT. 4th
Lect	Lectionaries
LXX	Greek Septuagint. 3rd/2nd BC
M 021	Campianus. 9th
Mac/Sym	patristic: Macarius/Symeon. 4th/5th
mae	Middle Egyptian Coptic version
Marc	patristic: Marcus Eremita. 430 AD
Mcion	patristic: Marcion. 2nd
Meth	patristic: Methodius of Olympus. 250 AD
mf	Middle Fayyumic Coptic (/cw)
Ms	Manuscript
Mss	Manuscripts
MT	Masoretic Text
N 022	Petropolitanus Purpureus. 6th
Nic	patristic: Nicetas of Remesiana. 414 AD
Nil	patristic: Nilus of Ancyra. 430 AD
OL	Old Latin, Vetus Latina
Omega 045	Athous Dionysiou. 9th
Or	patristic: Origen. 254 AD
P^e 024	Guelferbytanus A. 6th
p4	3rd
p11	6th
p13	3rd/4th
p16	3rd/4th
p40	3rd
p44	6th/7th
p45	3rd
p46	c. 200 AD
p47	3rd
p61	c. 700 AD
p66	c. 200 AD

p72	3rd/4th
p74	7th
p75	3rd
p88	4th
p100	3rd/4th
p115	3rd/4th
p124	6th
pbo	Proto-Bohairic Coptic 4th/5th
Pel	patristic: Pelagius. 418 AD
PetA	patristic: Peter of Alexandria. 311 AD
PH	Paleo-Hebrew
Phi 028	Beratinus. 6th
Philo-Car	patristic: Philo-Carpasia. 4th
Pi 041	Petropolitanus. 9th
Prim	patristic: Primasius of Hadrumetum. 567 AD
Psi 044	Athous Lavrensis. c. 8th/9th
Ruf	patristic: Rufinus of Aquileia. 410 AD
S 028	Vaticanus 354. 949 AD
sa	Sahidic Coptic version. 3rd/4th
Ser	patristic: Serapion of Thmuis. 362 AD
slav	Slavonic version. 10th/11th
SP	Samaritan Pentateuch. c. 1100 AD
Spec	patristic: Speculum. 5th
Symmachus	Symmachus (translator). Late 2nd
syr	Entire Syriac tradition
syr(c)	Syriac Curetonianus. 5th
syr(h)	Syriac Harklensis. 616 AD
syr(p)	Syriac Peshitta. 5th/6th
syr(pal)	Syriac Palestinian. 6th
syr(ph)	Syriac Philoxeniana. 507/508 AD
syr(s)	Syriac Sinaiticus. c. 4th
T 029	Borgianus. 5th
Tert	patristic: Tertullian. 220 AD
Tg	Aramaic Targum.
Theod	patristic: Theodore of Mopsuestia. 428 AD
Theoph	patristic: Theophilus of Alexandria. 412 AD

TheoHer	patristic: Theodore-Heraclea. 358 AD
Theta 038	Coridethianus. 9th
Thret	patristic: Theodoret of Cyrus. 466 AD
Tit	patristic: Titus of Bostra. 378 AD
U 030	Nanianus. 9th
V031	Mosquensis II. 9th
Var	patristic: Varimadum. 5th
vg	Latin Vulgate of Jerome c. 400 AD
vid	ut videtur: probable but uncertain
Vig	patristic: Vigilius of Thapsus. 484 AD
W 032	Washingtonianus. 5th
X 033	Monacensis. 9th/10th
Y 034	Macedoniensis. 9th
Z 035	Dublinensis. 6th
046	10th
048	5th
049	9th
056	10th
058	4th
067	6th
073	6th
075	10th
078	6th
081	Tischendorfianus II. 6th
083	5th/6th
0102	7th
0104	6th
0106	Tischendorfianus I. 7th
0107	7th
0122	10th
0141	10th
0142	10th
0150	9th
0208	6th
0211	7th
0233	8th

0250	Climaci Rescriptus.	8th
0274		5th
0278		9th
0279		8th/9th
0281		7th/8th
0285		6th
0300		6th/7th

Acknowledgments

I would like to thank Dr G. Mhuriyashe Mushayabasa, Researcher in Semitic Languages, North-West University, South Africa, for his assistance in some of the retroversions from Syriac, Aramaic and Greek to Biblical Hebrew.

Introduction

The era of hand copying of Biblical manuscripts spans from approximately 1450 BC to 1450 AD, from Moses and the first Biblical manuscripts to the time of the first printing press.[1] The text that has generally been used for the Old Testament is known as the Masoretic text (MT), as represented by Codex Leningradensis of 1009 AD, the oldest complete manuscript of the Hebrew portion of the Bible. The Greek New Testament is largely based on copies beginning from the early 2nd century and is a product of comparing all the known manuscripts using the discipline known as textual criticism.

In the human enterprise of hand copying, mistakes are likely, and ancient texts that were copied by hand accumulated errors during their copying history. Even modern printed editions have errors, even after several proof readings. It has therefore been the goal of the Biblical text critic to examine the extant manuscript copies in order to recover and preserve the authentic text.[2]

The script around the time of Moses and the first Biblical scrolls was the early West Semitic (or Proto-Canaanite[3]) consonantal writing system, the parent of the Paleo-Hebrew script. This proto-alphabet originated in the Middle Bronze Age (MBA) and uses the Semitic (rather than the Egyptian) word for the object of the pictograph, and was developed using the principle of acrophony to assign phonetic values to its approximate 28 characters (mostly borrowed Egyptian hieroglyphs). In contrast, the Babylonian and Egyptian systems required hundreds of signs. The new alphabetic script was the simplest that the region had known.

While it has been thought that the proto-alphabet was invented by Canaanite workers[4] in Egypt during the XIIth Dynasty, there is evidence that the script had earlier beginnings at Byblos (Gubla), from its contacts in the late 3rd millennium BC with Egypt and Ebla.[5]

The syllabic script used at Byblos and elsewhere during the MBA had a right to left direction and characters that look like modified common Egyptian hieroglyphs. About 18 of the signs have counterparts in the 22 letters of the Phoenician alphabet, and many of the characters seem to be derived from Old Kingdom hieratic, probably from trade Egypt had with Byblos for timber in the 3rd millennium BC.

The proto-alphabet may have been developed as a simplification of the Proto-Byblian syllabary in a move from syllabic to consonantal writing in the style of the Egyptian script.[6] Whether the alphabet originated at Byblos or in Egypt for its Canaanite population is unclear.

By the end of the Bronze Age in the Levant, the three West Semitic writing systems of syllabary, consonantary, and cuneiform were still in use. At the beginning of the Iron Age, the early Phoenician alphabet appeared c. 1200-1050 BC, consisting of 22 letters written right to left. The Proto-Hebrew script at this time was very similar to the Phoenician with only minor differences. By convention both scripts are called Proto-Canaanite. By the beginning of the 10th century BC the script in Israel is known as Paleo-Hebrew.

After the Babylonian exile in the 6th century BC, a transition occurred to a form of the Assyrian script which used the Phoenician alphabet. Approximately three centuries later a stylized form of Aramaic similar to the script used by the Persian Empire, known as Jewish Square Script, began to be used. The Hebrew scripts among the Dead Sea Scrolls include Paleo-Hebrew and Square Script.

Approximately 90% of the Dead Sea Scrolls were written on vellum, a parchment made of processed calf hide, with the remaining 10% written on papyrus. The scribes of the scrolls used reed pens to write, made from dried reeds which were cut to a point and then slit at the end. The black ink used on the scrolls was found to be carbon black from olive oil lamps, thinned out with ingredients such as honey, oil, vinegar and water for proper consistency of writing.

In text criticism, one of the more common types of copying mistake is known as haplography, which occurs when something is written once that occurs two or more times in the original. It is also known as parablepsis, which means 'a looking to the side.' It occurs when letters are repeated in a text and there is a skip to another occurrence. This type of mistake happened not only in Hebrew scripts but also in the translations of Syriac, Aramaic, Greek and Latin.

If the haplography involves the beginning letters it is known as homoioarcton. If the letters involved are at the end of the word it is termed homoioteleuton. There are also instances where the same word is written twice in a row and the first drops out in a skip to the second one, which is known as homoiologon. If the letter or word involved in the skip only looks similar it is called sight or graphic confusion.[7] And if the skip was to a letter or word that sounds similar, it is known as aural or sound confusion. Also among copying errors is dittography, the unintentional repetition of letters or words.[8] The most common causes of textual corruption are accidental rather than intentional.

When reading commentaries on the books of the Bible one will notice that some include discussion of the manuscripts along with text critical notes, and sometimes noted is a word or words which fell out in manuscripts and in certain textual streams and have not as yet been restored back to any Bible. In fact, the list of such words has grown fairly long, and the primary reason can be traced to an unbalanced use of a tool in text criticism known as lectio brevior, or "the shortest reading is preferable."

Those who have studied haplography in the manuscripts have duly noted the problem: "[A]lthough haplography is recognized conceptually by all text critics, when it comes to the analysis of specific passages, it is largely dismissed."[9]

The solution to the disparity often encountered in text critical analysis of shorter texts has been noted by the same investigators: "Because of the prevalence of mistakes in every known manuscript, we feel that due consideration should be given to the possibility of scribal oversight when explaining a variant *before* resorting to any theory based on intentional alteration."[10]

In this study, the possibility of scribal oversight as explanation of a shorter reading was given appropriate consideration before any appeal to deliberate modification.

In the analysis of MT for words lost from scribal haplography, MT Mss, MT Qere, Cairo Geniza, Dead Sea Scrolls, Samaritan Pentateuch, Syriac Peshitta, Targum, Septuagint, Vetus Latina and Vulgate were consulted, as well as consideration of text critical literature.

When manuscripts in a language other than Hebrew had additional words not found in MT, the extra words were translated to Biblical Hebrew in a process known as retroversion, a reconstruction of the parent Hebrew text based on the words used in the translation. This was done in order to determine if the extra words represented text lost from haplography in other manuscripts, or were later scribal expansions. The Hebrew text was sometimes examined in earlier Square Scripts as well as Paleo-Hebrew scripts for any evidence of haplography.

For the New Testament (NT) the Biblical manuscripts were consulted and a comparison was made with the Nestle-Aland Novum Testamentum Graece, 28th revised edition, along with several other Greek NT editions,[11] the Latin Vulgate of Jerome,[12] and Codex Sinaiticus, the earliest complete Greek NT manuscript.

A subsequent haplography list with verses in English and corresponding Hebrew or Greek with manuscript notes[13] was compiled. The letters or words involved in the scribal haplography for each case were underlined and the words that dropped out were bracketed so that the text involved in the skip can be readily identified.

It is hoped that after the list is read that the reader will be able to say with a significant degree of confidence that they have finally read the *whole* Bible!

NOTES

[1] The first finished copies of the Latin Gutenberg Bible were available in 1454, while the first printing of the Hebrew Tanakh took place on February 23, 1488, and the first Greek NT edition on March 1, 1516.

[2] P. K. McCarter, Textual Criticism, 12.

[3] Also termed Proto-Sinaitic, since its first discovery in the Sinai, but the script has also been found in Egypt at a site between Thebes and Abydos, and in the Levant.

[4] O. Goldwasser, Canaanites Reading Hieroglyphs, Ägypten und Levante XVI, 121-60.

[5] M. V. Tonietti, The Assyrian model, in Origins of the Alphabet. Proceedings of the First Polis Institute Interdisciplinary Conference, 49-72.

[6] B. E. Colless, The Origin of the Alphabet, Antiguo Oriente 12, 80, 94. Also, a monumental inscription found at Byblos has a script that seems intermediate between Proto-Byblian and the later Phoenician alphabet, and may provide a link to early Phoenician. Another hypothesis is that Proto-Sinaitic developed into Proto-Canaanite in the LBA and then into Phoenician. Cf. J. F. Healey, The early alphabet, 18. The use of Old Kingdom hieratic in the Proto-Byblian syllabary is one argument for its origin in the late EB III.

[7] This has also been termed virtual haplography.

[8] J. F. Brug, Textual Criticism of the Old Testament, 11-22.

[9] N. Freedman and D. Miano, Slip of the Eye, in The Challenge of Bible Translation, 283.

[10] Freedman and Miano, Slip of the Eye, 283; Cf. also E. Tov, Textual Criticism of the Hebrew Bible, 306.

[11] Novum Instrumentum omne. Edited by Desiderius Erasmus, 1516; The New Testament in the Original Greek According to the Text Followed in the

Authorized Version. Edited by F. H. A. Scrivener. Cambridge, 1894; Novum Testamentum Graece, 8th edition. Edited by Konstantinus Tischendorf. Lipsiae: Giesecke & Devrient, 1872; The New Testament in the Original Greek, by Brooke Foss Westcott and Fenton John Anthony Hort, 1881; The New Testament in the Original Greek: Byzantine Text Form. Compiled and arranged by Maurice A. Robinson and William G. Pierpont, 2005; Society of Biblical Literature SBL Greek New Testament, 2010.

[12] Novum Testamentum Domini Nostri Iesu Christi Latine Secundum Editionem Sancti Hieronymi. Edited by J. Wordsworth, H. J. White, et al., 1889-1954. vg(ww); Biblia Sacra Iuxta Vulgatam Versionem. Edited by B. Fischer, J. Gribomont, et al., 2007. vg(st).

[13] Greek OT: LXX Septuaginta. Edited by A. Rahlfs. Württembergische Bibelanstalt / Deutsche Bibelgesellschaft, Stuttgart; Septuaginta: Vetus Testamentum Graecum. Gottingen: Vandenhoeck & Ruprecht; The Old Testament in Greek. Edited by A. E. Brooke and N. McLean. Cambridge University Press. Hebrew OT: Biblia Hebraica Stuttgartensia, 5th edition. Edited by K. Elliger and W. Rudolph. Deutsche Bibelgesellschaft, 1997; The Biblical Qumran Scrolls: Transcriptions and Textual Variants. Edited by E. Ulrich. Supplements to Vetus Testamentum, 134. Leiden: Brill, 2010; Greek NT: Nestle-Aland Novum Testamentum Graece, 28th edition. Deutsche Bibelgesellschaft, 2012. 3rd Corrected Printing, 2014; The Center for New Testament Textual Studies NT Critical Apparatus. New Orleans Baptist Theological Seminary, 2004.

Haplography List: Old Testament

Genesis 1:6 LXX(H) OL (MT restored in v.7)
למים [וַיְהִי כֵן]: וַיַּעַשׂ

Genesis 1:6 And God said, "Let there be an expanse in the middle of the waters, and let it divide the waters from the waters." [And it was so.]

Genesis 1:8 LXX(H) OL
שמים [וַיַּרְא אלהים כי טוב] וַיְהִי

Genesis 1:8 And God called the expanse sky. [And God saw that it was good.] And there was evening and there was morning, a second day.

Genesis 1:9 DSS Ms LXX OL
ויאמר אלהים יקוו המים מתחת השמים אל מקום אחד ותראה היבשה ויהי כן [וַיִּקָווּ המים מתחת השמים אל מקויהם ותראה היבשה]: וַיִּקְרָא

Genesis 1:9 And God said, "Let the waters under the sky be gathered together in one gathering, and let the dry land appear." And it was so. [And the waters under the sky gathered to their gatherings, and the dry land appeared.]

Genesis 1:20 LXX(H) OL
השמים [וַיְהִי כֵן]: וַיִּבְרָא

Genesis 1:20 And God said, "Let the waters swarm with swarms of living creatures, and let birds fly above the earth in the open expanse of sky." [And it was so.]

Genesis 2:20 LXX(H) Syr Tg Ms Vg
הבהמה וּלַ[כֹל] עוף השמים

Genesis 2:20 The man gave names to all the livestock, and to [all] the birds of the sky, and to every wild animal of the field; but for man there was not found a helper suitable for him.

Genesis 7:2 SP LXX Syr Vg
טהרה היא <u>שנים</u> [<u>שנים</u>] איש ואשתו

Genesis 7:2 You shall take seven pairs of every clean animal with you, the male and his female. Of the animals that are not clean, take two [and two], the male and his female.

Genesis 7:3 LXX(H)
שבעה <u>זכר ונקבה</u> [ומכל העוף איננה טהרה שנים שנים <u>זכר ונקבה</u>] לחיות

Genesis 7:3 Also of the clean birds of the sky, seven and seven, a male and a female, [and of all the unclean birds, two and two, a male and a female], to preserve their offspring on the surface of all the earth.

Genesis 10:24 LXX(H)
וארפכשד <u>ילד את</u> [קינן וקינן <u>ילד את</u>] שלח ושלח ילד את עבר

Genesis 10:24 And Arpachshad became the father of [Kenan. And Kenan became the father of] Shelah. And Shelah became the father of Eber.

(Genesis 1 with restorations)

Genesis

1 In the beginning God created the heavens and the earth. ²Now the earth was formless and empty. Darkness was on the surface of the deep. God's Spirit was hovering over the surface of the waters.

³And God said, "Let there be light," and there was light. ⁴And God saw the light, and saw that it was good. God divided the light from the darkness. ⁵And God called the light Day, and the darkness he called Night. There was evening and there was morning, one day.

⁶And God said, "Let there be an expanse in the middle of the waters, and let it divide the waters from the waters." And it was so. ⁷And God made the expanse, and divided the waters which were under the expanse from the waters which were above the expanse. ⁸And God called the expanse Sky. And God saw that it was good. There was evening and there was morning, a second day.

⁹And God said, "Let the waters under the sky be gathered together in one gathering, and let the dry land appear." And it was so. And the waters under the sky gathered to their gatherings, and the dry land appeared. ¹⁰And God called the dry land Earth,

and the gathering together of the waters he called Seas. And God saw that it was good. ¹¹And God said, "Let the earth produce vegetation, plants yielding seed, and fruit trees bearing fruit after their kind, with its seed in it, on the earth." And it was so.

¹²And the earth brought forth vegetation, plants yielding seed after their kind, and trees bearing fruit, with its seed in it, after their kind. And God saw that it was good. ¹³And there was evening and there was morning, a third day. ¹⁴And God said, "Let there be lights in the expanse of the sky to divide the day from the night; and let them be for signs, and for seasons, and for days and for years; ¹⁵and let them be for lights in the expanse of sky to give light on the earth." And it was so.

¹⁶And God made the two great lights: the greater light to rule the day, and the lesser light to rule the night. He also made the stars. ¹⁷And God set them in the expanse of sky to give light to the earth, ¹⁸and to rule over the day and over the night, and to divide the light from the darkness. God saw that it was good. ¹⁹And there was evening and there was morning, a fourth day.

²⁰And God said, "Let the waters swarm with swarms of living creatures, and let birds fly above the earth in the open expanse of sky." And it was so. ²¹And God created the large sea creatures, and every living creature that moves, with which the waters swarmed, after their kind, and every winged bird after its kind. And God saw that it was good. ²²And God blessed them, saying, "Be fruitful, and multiply, and fill the waters in the seas, and let birds multiply on the earth." ²³There was evening and there was morning, a fifth day.

²⁴And God said, "Let the earth bring forth living creatures after their kind, livestock, creeping things, and animals of the earth after their kind." And it was so. ²⁵And God made the animals of the earth after their kind, and the livestock after their kind, and everything that creeps on the ground after its kind. God saw that it was good.

²⁶And God said, "Let us make man in our image, after our likeness: and let them have dominion over the fish of the sea, and over the birds of the sky, and over the livestock, and over all the earth, and over every creeping thing that creeps on the earth." ²⁷And God created man in his own image. In God's image he created him; male and female he created them.

²⁸And God blessed them. God said to them, "Be fruitful, multiply, fill the earth, and subdue it. Have dominion over the fish of the sea, over the birds of the sky, and over every living thing that moves on the earth."

²⁹And God said, "Behold, I have given you every plant yielding seed, which is on the surface of all the earth, and every tree, which bears fruit yielding seed. It will be your food. ³⁰And to every animal of the earth, and to every bird of the sky, and to everything that creeps on the earth, in which there is life, I have given every green plant for food." And it was so.

³¹And God saw everything that he had made, and, behold, it was very good. There was evening and there was morning, a sixth day.

Genesis 11:13 LXX(H)
ויחי ארפכשד אחרי הולידו את קינן שלשים שנים וארבע
מאות שנה ויולד בנים ובנות [ויחי קינן שלשים שנה ומאת
שנה ויולד את ושלח ויחי קינן אחרי הולידו את שלח שלשים
שנים ושלש מאות שנה ויולד בנים ובנית] ושלח

Genesis 11:13 And Arpachshad lived after he became the father of Kenan thirty and four hundred years, and fathered sons and daughters. [And Kenan lived thirty and a hundred years, and became the father of Shelah. And Kenan lived after he had become the father of Shelah thirty years and three hundred years, and fathered sons and daughters.]

Genesis 12:17 LXX(H)
נגעים גדלים [ורעים] ואת ביתו

Genesis 12:17 The LORD plagued Pharaoh and his house with great [and grievous] plagues because of Sarai, Abram's wife.

Genesis 22:1 Hebrew Mss LXX Vg Mss
אליו אברהם [אברהם] ויאמר הנני

Genesis 22:1 It happened after these things, that God tested Abraham, and said to him, "Abraham, [Abraham.]" And he said, "Here I am."

Genesis 24:22 SP LXX Mss
משקלו [וישם על אפה] ושני

Genesis 24:22 It happened, as the camels had finished drinking, that the man took a gold ring weighing a beka, [which he put on her nose,] and two bracelets for her hands of ten (shekels) weight of gold,

Genesis 31:44 LXX(H)
לעד ביני ובינך [ויאמר הנה אין איש עמנו ראה אלהים עד ביני ובינך]

Genesis 31:44 Now come, let us make a covenant, you and I; and let it be a witness between me and you." [And he said to him, "Behold, there is no one with us; see, God is witness between me and you."]

Genesis 37:9 LXX(H)
ויספר אתו [לאָבִיו] וְלְאֶחָיו

Genesis 37:9 And he dreamed yet another dream, and told it [to his father] and to his brothers, and said, "Behold, I have dreamed yet another dream; and behold, the sun and the moon and eleven stars bowed down to me."

Genesis 39:4 SP LXX Vg
בעיניו [אדניו] וישרת

Genesis 39:4 So Joseph found favor in the sight [of his master], and served him, and he made him overseer over his house, and all that he had he put into his hand.

Genesis 39:17 LXX(H) OL
לצחק בי [וַיֹאמר לי אשכב עמך]: וַיְהִי

Genesis 39:17 She spoke to him according to these words, saying, "The Hebrew servant, whom you have brought to us, came in to me to mock me, [and said to me, "Let me lie with you."]

Genesis 43:26 LXX(H) Vg
וישתחוו לו [אַפִּים] אַרצה

Genesis 43:26 When Joseph came home, they brought him the present which was in their hand into the house, and bowed themselves down to him [with their face] to the ground.

Genesis 43:28 SP LXX
חי [וַיֹאמר ברוך האיש ההוא לאלהים] וַיִקְדו

Genesis 43:28 They said, "Your servant, our father, is well. He is still alive." [And he said, "Blessed be that man by God."] And they bowed and prostrated themselves.

Genesis 47:5 LXX(H) (MT partially restored () in v.6)
ויאמר פרעה אל־יוסף לאמר [(ישבו בארץ גשן ואם ידעת
ויש בם אנשי חיל ושמתם שרי מקנה על אשר לי) ויבאו
מצרים אל־יוסף יעקב ובניו וישמע פרעה מלך מצרים
ויאמר פרעה אל־יוסף לאמר] אביך ואחיך באו אליך:

Genesis 47:5 And Pharaoh spoke to Joseph, saying, [("Let them dwell in the land of Goshen. If you know any able men among them, then put them in charge of my livestock.") So Jacob and his sons came into Egypt to Joseph, and Pharaoh, king of Egypt, heard of it. And Pharaoh spoke to Joseph, saying,] "Your father and your brothers have come to you.

Genesis 47:16 SP LXX Syr
ואתנה לכם [לחם] במקניכם

Genesis 47:16 Joseph said, "Give me your livestock; and I will give you [food] for your livestock, if your money is gone."

Genesis 48:1 LXX(H)
ואת אפרים [ויבא אל יעקב]: ויגד ליעקב

Genesis 48:1 It happened after these things, that someone said to Joseph, "Behold, your father is sick." And taking with him his two sons, Manasseh and Ephraim, [he went to Jacob]. 2 And someone...

Genesis 48:21 LXX(H)
והשיב אתכם [אלהים מן הארץ הזאת] אל ארץ אבתיכם

Genesis 48:21 And Israel said to Joseph, "Behold, I am dying, but God will be with you, and [from this land God] will bring you back to the land of your fathers.

Exodus 2:14 LXX(H)
הרגת [אתמול] את המצרי

Exodus 2:14 He said, "Who made you a prince and a judge over us? Do you plan to kill me, as you killed the Egyptian [yesterday]?" Moses was afraid, and said, "Surely this thing is known."

Exodus 2:17 LXX(H)
משה ויושען [וידל להן] וישק

Exodus 2:17 The shepherds came and drove them away; but Moses stood up and helped them, [and drew water for them,] and watered their flock.

Exodus 2:21 SP LXX
בתו לַמשֶׁה [לָאשָׁה]: ותלד בן

Exodus 2:21 And Moses was content to dwell with the man. And he gave Moses Zipporah his daughter [in marriage].

Exodus 3:16 DSS LXX SP Syr
את זקנֵי [בנֵי] ישראל

Exodus 3:16 Go, and gather the elders of [the children of] Israel together, and tell them, 'The LORD, the God of your fathers, the God of Abraham, of Isaac, and of Jacob, has appeared to me, saying, "I have surely visited you, and seen that which is done to you in Egypt;

Exodus 8:5(1) LXX(H)
אל אַהֲרן [אָחִיךָ] נטה

Exodus 8:5 The LORD said to Moses, "Tell Aaron [your brother], 'Stretch forth your hand with your rod over the rivers, over the streams, and over the pools, and cause frogs to come up on the land of Egypt.'"

Exodus 8:16(12) DSS SP LXX
נטה את [ידְךָ] במטךָ והך את עפר

Exodus 8:16 The LORD said to Moses, "Tell Aaron, 'Stretch out [your hand] with your rod, and strike the dust of the earth, that it may become lice throughout all the land of Egypt.'"

Exodus 9:28 DSS LXX
וברד [וָאש] וַאשלחה

Exodus 9:28 Pray to the LORD; for there has been enough of God's thunder and hail [and fire]. I will let you go, and you shall stay no longer."

Exodus 10:24 DSS MT Mss LXX Syr Ms Tg Ms Vg
אל משה [ולאהרן] ויאמרו

Exodus 10:24 Then Pharaoh called to Moses [and to Aaron] and said, "Go, serve the LORD. Only let your flocks and your herds stay behind. Let your little ones also go with you."

Exodus 20:12 Nash Pap. LXX(H)
כבד את אביך ואת אמל <u>למען</u> [ייטב לך ולמען] יארכון

Exodus 20:12 "Honor your father and your mother, that [it may be well with you, that] your days may be long in the land which the LORD your God gives you.

Exodus 22:5(4) (SP) LXX(H)
ב<u>שדה</u> אח<u>ר</u> [שלם ישלם משדהו כתבואתה ואם כל ה<u>שדה</u> יבע<u>ר</u>] מיטב

Exodus 22:5 "... another man's field, [he shall make restitution from his own field according to his produce; and if he shall have grazed over the whole field,] he shall make restitution from the best of his own field, and from the best of his own vineyard.

Exodus 22:20 LXX(H) Mss Syr
לאלה<u>ים</u> [אחר<u>ים</u>] יחרם

Exodus 22:20 He who sacrifices to [another] god, except to the LORD only, shall be utterly destroyed.

Exodus 29:38 SP LXX
ליום <u>תמיד</u> [עלת <u>תמיד</u>] את הכבש

Exodus 29:38 "Now this is that which you shall offer on the altar: two lambs a year old day by day continually, [a continual burnt offering].

Exodus 40:18 DSS
וישם [את קרסיו] ואת קרשיו

Exodus 40:18 And Moses erected the tabernacle, and put its sockets in place, and set up [its hooks and] its boards, and put in its bars, and he erected its pillars.

Leviticus 10:1 DSS LXX
ויקחו [שני] בני אהרן

Leviticus 10:1 And the [two] sons of Aaron, Nadab and Abihu, each took his censer and put fire in it, and laid incense on it, and offered strange fire before the LORD, which he had not commanded them.

Leviticus 15:3 (DSS) SP LXX
זובו או החתים בשרו מזובו [טמא הוא כל ימי זב
בשרו או החתים בשרו מזובו] טמאתו היא:

Leviticus 15:3 This shall be his uncleanness in his discharge: whether his body runs with his discharge, or his body has stopped from his discharge, [it is his uncleanness. All the days of the discharge of his body, even if his body obstructs his discharge,] it is his uncleanness.

Leviticus 17:4 DSS Ms SP LXX
ואל פתח אהל מועד לא הביאו [לעשות אתו עלה או
שלמים ליהוה לרצונכם לריח ניחח וישחטהו בחוץ
ואל פתח אהל מועד לא הביאו] להקריב

Leviticus 17:4 and hasn't brought it to the door of the Tent of Meeting, [so as to sacrifice it for a burnt offering or peace offering to the LORD to be acceptable as a soothing aroma, and whoever shall kill it outside, and shall not bring it to the door of the Tent of Meeting] to offer it as an offering to the LORD before the tabernacle of the LORD, blood shall be imputed to that man. He has shed blood; and that man shall be cut off from among his people.

Leviticus 22:18 DSS Hebrew Mss SP Syr Vg
ומן הגר [הגר] בישראל

Leviticus 22:18 "Speak to Aaron, and to his sons, and to all the children of Israel, and say to them, 'Any man of the house of Israel or the sojourners [who sojourn] in Israel, who offers his offering, whether it be any of their vows, or any of their freewill offerings, which they offer to the LORD for a burnt offering;

Numbers 4:7 DSS(4QLXXNum)(H)
הנסך [להם] ולחם התמיד

Numbers 4:7 On the table of show bread they shall spread a blue cloth, and put on it the dishes, the spoons, the bowls, and the pitchers for pouring [with them]; and the continual bread shall be on it.

Numbers 14:12 SP LXX
ואעשה אתך [ואת בית אביך] לגוי גדול

Numbers 14:12 I will strike them with pestilence, and disinherit them, and I will make you [and your father's house] a nation greater and mightier than they."

Numbers 23:3 DSS LXX
יאמר בלעם לבלק התיצב על עלתך ואלכה אולי וקרה
אלוהים לקראתי ודבר מה יראני והגדתי לך וילך [ויתיצב
בלק על עולתו ובלעם נקרה אל אלוהים וילך] שפי

Numbers 23:3 Balaam said to Balak, "Station yourself by your burnt offering, and I will go. Perhaps God will come to meet me, and whatever he shows me I will tell you." [And Balak went off and stationed himself by his offering, and Balaam called to God] and went off to a barren height.

Numbers 25:16 DSS LXX
וידבר יהוה אל משה לאמר [דבר לבני ישראל לאמר]: הננו

Numbers 25:16 And the LORD spoke to Moses, saying, ["Speak to the children of Israel, saying,]

Numbers 36:1 DSS LXX Syr
לפני משה [ולפני אלעזר הכהן] ולפני הנשאים ראשי אבות לבני ישראל

Numbers 36:1 The heads of the ancestral houses of the family of the children of Gilead, the son of Machir, the son of Manasseh, of the families of the sons of Joseph, came near and spoke before Moses [and before Eleazar the priest] and before the leaders, the heads of the ancestral houses of the children of Israel.

Deuteronomy 2:13 SP LXX
עתה קמו [סעו] ועברו לכם

Deuteronomy 2:13 "Now rise up, [depart,] and cross over the Wadi Zered." So we crossed the Wadi Zered.

Deuteronomy 4:28 Hebrew Mss LXX
אלהים [אחרים] מעשה

Deuteronomy 4:28 There you shall serve [other] gods, the work of men's hands, wood and stone, which neither see, nor hear, nor eat, nor smell.

Deuteronomy 4:33 SP LXX
קול אלהים [חיים] מדבר

Deuteronomy 4:33 Did a people ever hear the voice of [the living] God speaking out of the midst of the fire, as you have heard, and live?

Deuteronomy 5:27 DSS Ms + Syr LXX Mss Vg
אלהינו [אליכה] ואת תדבר

Deuteronomy 5:27 Go near, and hear all that the LORD our God shall say [to you], and tell us all that the LORD our God speaks to you; and we will hear it, and do it."

Deuteronomy 6:13 Hebrew Mss LXX
תעבד [ובו תדבק] ובשמו

Deuteronomy 6:13 You shall fear the LORD your God; and you shall serve him only, [and you shall cling to him,] and take oaths by his name.

Deuteronomy 7:15 DSS LXX
מצרים הרעים אשר [ראיתה ואשר] ידעת

Deuteronomy 7:15 And the LORD will take away from you all sickness, and none of the evil diseases of Egypt, which [you have seen and which] you have known, will he put on you, but he will lay them on all who hate you.

Deuteronomy 8:7 DSS LXX SP
טובה [ורחבה] ארץ

Deuteronomy 8:7 For the LORD your God brings you into a good [and spacious] land, a land of brooks of water, of springs, and underground water flowing into valleys and hills;

Deuteronomy 11:8 DSS LXX
תחזקו [ורביתם] ובאתם

Deuteronomy 11:8 Therefore you shall keep every commandment which I command you this day, that you may be strong, [and multiply,] and go in and possess the land, where you go over to possess it;

Deuteronomy 12:28 SP LXX
שמר וַשמעתַ [וַעשיתַ] את כל הדברים

Deuteronomy 12:28 Observe and hear [and do] all these words which I command you, that it may go well with you, and with your children after you forever, when you do that which is good and right in the eyes of the LORD your God.

Deuteronomy 13:6(7) DSS SP LXX
כי יסיתך אחיך [בן אביך או] בן אמך

Deuteronomy 13:6 If your brother, [the son of your father, or] the son of your mother, or your son, or your daughter, or the wife you embrace, or your friend who is closest to you, entice you secretly, saying, "Let us go and serve other gods," which you have not known, you, nor your fathers;

Deuteronomy 30:14 DSS LXX
ובלבבך [ובידך] לעשתו

Deuteronomy 30:14 But the word is very near to you; it is in your mouth and in your heart [and in your hand], so that you can do it.

Deuteronomy 30:16 LXX(H) (cf. PH)
ואת הרע: [אִם תשמע אל מצות יהוה אלהיך] אֲשֶׁר אנכי

Deuteronomy 30:16 [If you obey the commandments of the LORD your God] that I command you this day, to love the LORD your God, to walk in his ways, and to keep his commandments and his statutes and his ordinances, then you will live and multiply, and the LORD your God will bless you in the land where you are going to possess it.

Deuteronomy 31:28 DSS LXX
שבטיכם [וזקניכם ושפטיכם] ושטריכם

Deuteronomy 31:28 Assemble to me all the elders of your tribes, [and your elders and your judges] and your officers, that I may speak these words in their ears, and call heaven and earth to witness against them.

Deuteronomy 32:15 SP LXX
חמר: [וַיֹּאכַל יַעקב וישבע] וַיִּשְׁמַן יְשֻׁרוּן

Deuteronomy 32:15 [But Jacob ate his fill.] Jeshurun grew fat, and kicked. You have grown fat. You have grown thick. You have become sleek. Then he forsook God who made him, and lightly esteemed the Rock of his salvation.

Deuteronomy 32:43 DSS LXX: > MT
הרנינו [שמים עמו וישתחוו לו כל בני אלהים הרנינו] גוים

Deuteronomy 32:43 LXX(H): > DSS (MT)
מלאכי אֱלֹהִים [הרנינו גוים את עמו ויחזקו לו כל מלאכי אֱלֹהִים] כי

Deuteronomy 32:43 DSS+LXX(H)
הרנינו [שמים עמו והשתחוו לו כל מלאכי אלהים הרנינו]
גוים עמו [ויחזקו לו כל מלאכי אלהים] כי דם בניו יקום וְנָקָם
[וְנָקָם] ישיב לצריו [ולמשנאיו ישלם] וַיְכַפֵּר אדמת עמו

Deuteronomy 32:43 [Rejoice, O heavens, with him, and let all the angels of God worship him.] Rejoice, O nations, with his people, [and let all the angels of God strengthen themselves in him.] For he will avenge the blood of his sons, and he will render vengeance [and recompense justice] to his enemies, [and he will recompense them that hate him,] and he will cleanse the land for his people.

Deuteronomy 33:8 DSS LXX (sight confusion)
וללוי אמר [הבו ללוי] תֻמיך ואוריך

Deuteronomy 33:8 Of Levi he said, "[Give to Levi] your Thummim and your Urim to your godly man, whom you proved at Massah, with whom you strove at the waters of Meribah;

Joshua 2:1 LXX(H)
וילכו ויבאו [שני הנערים ליריחו ויבאו] בית אשה

Joshua 2:1 And Joshua the son of Nun secretly sent two young men out of Shittim as spies, saying, "Go, view the land, and Jericho." And they went and came [the two young men to Jericho, and entered] into the house of a prostitute whose name was Rahab, and slept there.

Joshua 4:5 LXX(H)
ויאמר להם יהושע עברו [לפָנַי] לפְנֵי ארון יהוה אלהיכם

Joshua 4:5 Joshua said to them, "Pass over [before me] in the presence of the ark of the LORD your God into the middle of the Jordan, and each of you pick up a stone and put it on your shoulder, according to the number of the tribes of the children of Israel;

Joshua 9:21 LXX(H) Mss
לכל העדה [ויעשו לכל העדה] כאשר

Joshua 9:21 And the leaders said to them, "Let them live." So they became wood cutters and drawers of water for all the congregation, [and all the congregation did] as the leaders had spoken to them.

Joshua 10:12 LXX(H)
את האמרי [ביד ישראל כי הכם בגבעון ויכון] לפני בני ישראל

Joshua 10:12 Then Joshua spoke to the LORD in the day when the LORD delivered up the Amorites [into the hand of Israel, when he struck them down at Gibeon, and they were struck down] before the children of Israel; and he said in the sight of Israel, "Sun, stand still on Gibeon. You, moon, stop in the valley of Aijalon."

Joshua 13:7-8 LXX(H)
וחצי השבט המנשה [מן הירדן עד הים הגדול מבוא השמש נתתם הים הגדול וגבל: 8 לשני המטות ולחצי השבט המנשה] עמו

Joshua 13:7 Now therefore divide this land for an inheritance to the nine tribes and the half-tribe of Manasseh: [from the Jordan as far as the great sea toward the setting of the sun, you are to give it; the great sea will be the boundary. 8 But to the two tribes and to the half-tribe of Manasseh,] with him the Reubenites and the Gadites received their inheritance, which Moses gave them, beyond the Jordan eastward, even as Moses the servant of the LORD gave them:

Joshua 15:59 LXX(H) OL
ערים שש וחצריהן [תקועה ואפרתה הוא בית לחם ופעור ועיטם וקולן ותתאם ושרש וכרם וגלים ובתר ומנוחה ערים אחת עשרה וחצריהן] קרית בעל

Joshua 15:59 and Maarath, and Beth Anoth, and Eltekon; six cities with their villages. [Tekoa, and Ephrathah (that is, Bethlehem), and Peor, and Etam, and Kolan, and Tatem, and Shoresh, and Kerem, and Gallim, and Bether and Manocho; eleven cities with their villages.]

Joshua 18:28 LXX(H)
וקרית [יערים] ערים

Joshua 18:28 And Zelah, Haeleph, and the Jebusite (that is, Jerusalem), Gibeath, and Kiriath [Jearim]; fourteen cities with their villages. This is the inheritance of the children of Benjamin according to their families.

Joshua 23:5 LXX(H)
אתם מלפניכם [עד אשר יאבדו ושלח בם את חית הסדה עד אשר ישמיד אותם ואט מלכיהם מפניכם] וירשתם

Joshua 23:5 And the LORD your God will himself thrust them out from before you, and drive them out of your sight, [and he will send wild animals against them until he utterly destroys them and their kings from before you;] and you will inherit their land, as the LORD your God spoke to you.

Judges 1:10 LXX(H)
היושב בחברון [ויצא חברון מנגד] ושם חברון לפנים

Judges 1:10 And Judah went against the Canaanites who lived in Hebron, [and Hebron came out in opposition] (now the name of Hebron before was Kiriath Arba), and they struck Sheshai, and Ahiman, and Talmai.

Judges 1:15 LXX(H)
ויתן לה כלב [כלבה] את גלת

Judges 1:15 She said to him, "Give me a blessing; since you have given me the land in the Negev, give me also springs of water." So Caleb gave her [according to her heart] the upper springs and the lower springs.

Judges 1:24 LXX(H)
מן העיר [ויקחו אתו] ויאמרו לו הראנו

Judges 1:24 And the spies saw a man coming out of the city, [and they captured him,] and they said to him, "Please show us the entrance into the city, and we will show you mercy."

Judges 2:19 LXX(H) Mss
ממעלליהם [ולא יסרו] מדרכם

Judges 2:19 But it happened, when the judge was dead, that they turned back, and dealt more corruptly than their fathers, in following other gods to serve them, and to bow down to them; they did not cease from their doings, [and they did not turn aside] from their stubborn way.

Judges 3:9 LXX(H)
הקטן ממנו [וישמע אליו]: ותהי עליו רוח

Judges 3:9 When the children of Israel cried to the LORD, the LORD raised up a savior to the children of Israel, who saved them, even Othniel the son of Kenaz, Caleb's younger brother; [and he obeyed him].

Judges 3:20 LXX(H)
לי אליך [המלך] ויקם מעל

Judges 3:20 Ehud came to him; and he was sitting by himself alone in the cool upper room. Ehud said, "I have a message from God for you, [O king]." And he rose from his seat.

Judges 3:21 LXX(H)
מעל הכסא: [ויהי ויקם] וישלח אהוד את יד

Judges 3:21 [And it happened as he rose up] that Ehud put forth his left hand and took the sword from his right thigh and thrust it into his belly.

Judges 3:30 LXX(H)
שמונים שנה [וישפט אותם אהוד עד מות]: ואחריו היה

Judges 3:30 So Moab was subdued that day under the hand of Israel. Then the land had rest eighty years. [And Ehud judged them till he died.]

Judges 5:12 LXX(H) Mss OL (cf. PH)
עורי עורי דבורה [עורי רבבות עם] עורי עורי דברי שיר [חזק]
קום ברק [וחזק דבורה ברק] ושבה שביך בן אבינעם

Judges 5:12 'Awake, awake, Deborah. [Awaken tens of thousands from among the people.] Awake, awake, sing a song. [Be strong.] Arise, Barak. [And Deborah, strengthen Barak.] And lead away your captives, son of Abinoam.'

Judges 6:5 LXX(H) Mss Cf. DSS OL
ואהליהם [וגמליהם] יבאו כדי ארבה לרב ולהם אין

Judges 6:5 For they came up with their livestock and their tents [and their camels]. They would come in like locusts in number, and they were innumerable. And they came into the land to ravage it.

Judges 6:14 LXX(H)
מכף מדיו [הנה] הלא שלחתיך

Judges 6:14 And the LORD looked at him, and said, "Go in this strength of yours and save Israel from the hand of Midian. [Behold,] haven't I sent you?"

Judges 8:11 LXX(H) Mss (sight confusion)
לנבח ויגבהֻה [נֹכח זבֻח] ויך את המחנה

Judges 8:11 And Gideon went up by the way of those who dwell in tents on the east of Nobah and Jogbehah, [opposite Zebah,] and struck the army, when the army was unsuspecting.

Judges 9:35 LXX(H)
ראשים: [וַיהי בבקר] וַיצא געל בן עבד

Judges 9:35 [And it happened early in the morning] that Gaal the son of Ebed went out, and stood in the entrance of the gate of the city. And Abimelech rose up, and the people who were with him, from the ambush.

Judges 11:7 LXX(H)
מבית אבי [וַתשלחוני מאתכם] וַמדוע באתם

Judges 11:7 Jephthah said to the elders of Gilead, "Did you not hate me, and drive me out of my father's house, [and sent me away from you]? And why have you come to me now when you are in distress?"

Judges 11:13 LXX(H)
אתהן בשלום [וַאלכה]: וַישובו המלאכים

Judges 11:13 And the king of the children of Ammon answered the messengers of Jephthah, "Because Israel took away my land, when he came up out of Egypt, from the Arnon even to the Jabbok, and to the Jordan. Now therefore restore it peaceably, [and I will depart]."

Judges 11:14 LXX(H) Mss OL
בשלום [וַישובו המלאכים אל יפתח] וַיסף עוד יפתח

Judges 11:14 [And the messengers returned to Jephthah,] and Jephthah sent messengers again to the king of the children of Ammon;

Judges 11:35 LXX(H) Mss
הכרע הכרעתַנִי [לְמִכְשָׁל הָיִית בְּעֵינַי] ואת היית

Judges 11:35 It happened, when he saw her, that he tore his clothes, and said, "Alas, my daughter. You have brought me very low. [You have become a stumbling block in my sight.] And you are among those who trouble me. For I have given my word to the LORD, and I can't break it."

Judges 12:2 LXX(H)
ובני עַמּוֹן [עִנּוּנִי] מאד ואזעק

Judges 12:2 And Jephthah said to them, "I and my people had a dispute, and the children of Ammon [were oppressing me] greatly; and when I called you, you did not save me out of their hand.

Judges 14:1 LXX(H) (cf. PH)
מבנות פלשתים [וַהִיא יָשְׁרָה בְעֵינָיו] וַיַּעַל וַיַּגֵּד

Judges 14:1 And Samson went down to Timnah, and saw a woman in Timnah of the daughters of the Philistines, [and she was right in his eyes].

Judges 14:5 LXX(H) Mss
ואמו תמנתה [וַיָּסַר] וַיָּבוֹא עד כרמי

Judges 14:5 Then Samson went down with his father and his mother to Timnah. [And he turned aside] and went into the vineyards of Timnah, and behold, a young lion roared against him.

Judges 15:6 Hebrew Mss LXX Syr
אותה ואֶת [בֵּית] אביה

Judges 15:6 Then the Philistines said, "Who has done this?" They said, "Samson, the son-in-law of the Timnite, because he has taken his wife, and given her to his companion." The Philistines came up, and burnt her and her father's [house] with fire.

Judges 16:1 LXX(H) (sight confusion PH)
וילך שמשון [מִשָּׁם] עזתה

Judges 16:1 And Samson went [from there] to Gaza, and saw a prostitute there, and went in to her.

Judges 16:3 LXX(H)
פני חברון [ויתנם שם]: וַיְהִי אחרי

Judges 16:3 Now Samson rested until midnight, but got up at midnight and took hold of the doors of the gate of the city, and the two posts, and pulled them up, bar and all, and put them on his shoulders, and carried them up to the top of the mountain that is overlooking Hebron, [and set them down there].

Judges 16:13-14 LXX(H)
את שבע מחלפות ראשי עם המסכת [ותקעת ביתד אל
הקיר וחליתי והייתי כאחד האדם ותישנהו ותארג
את שבע מחלפות ראשו עם המסכת] ותתקע

Judges 16:13-14a And Delilah said to Samson, "Until now, you have mocked me and told me lies. Tell me with what you might be bound." And he said to her, "If you weave the seven braids on my head with the web [and should fasten them with the pin to the wall, then I will be weak as another man." And it came to pass when he was asleep, that Delilah took the seven braids on his head and wove them with the web] and she fastened it with the pin, and said to him, "The Philistines are upon you, Samson..."

Judges 16:25 LXX(H) Mss
ויצחק לפניהם [ויכו אותו] וַיַעמידו אוֹתוֹ

Judges 16:25 And it happened, when their hearts were merry, that they said, "Call for Samson, that he may entertain us." So they called for Samson out of the prison, and he performed before them. [And they were striking him.] And they set him between the pillars;

Judges 16:26 LXX(H)
עליהם [ויעש הנער כן]: וַהבית

Judges 16:26 and Samson said to the boy who held him by the hand, "Allow me to feel the pillars on which the house rests, that I may lean on them." [And the boy did so.]

Judges 18:9 LXX(H) Mss OL
ויאמרו קוּמָה וְנַעֲלֶה עֲלֵיהֶם [כי עלינו ויסע בארץ עד לישה ויראו את העם אשר בקרבה יושבת לבטח כמשפט צדנים ורחקים המה מצדנים ודבר אין להם עם ארם כי קוּמָה וְנַעֲלֶה עֲלֵיהֶם] כי ראינו את הארץ

Judges 18:9 They said, "Arise, and let us go up against them; [for we have entered and journeyed in the land as far as Laish, and we saw the people how they lived in security, after the manner of the Sidonians, and they were far from the Sidonians, and they had no dealings with Aram. But arise, and let us go up against them;] for we have seen the land, and behold, it is very good. Will you do nothing? Do not hesitate to go and to enter in to possess the land.

Judges 18:20 LXX(H)
ואת הפסל [וְאֶת הַמַּסֵּכָה] וַיָּבֹא בקרב

Judges 18:20 And the priest's heart was glad, and he took the ephod, and the teraphim, and the engraved image, [and the molten image,] and went in the midst of the people.

Judges 18:22 LXX(H)
מבית מִיכָה [וְהִנֵּה מִיכָה] והאנשים אשר

Judges 18:22 They were some distance from the house of Micah, [and behold, Micah] and the men who were in the houses near Micah's house gathered together and overtook the children of Dan.

Judges 18:24 LXX(H) Vg
אשר עָשִׂיתִי [לִי] לַקַחְתֶּם

Judges 18:24 He said, "You have taken away my gods which I made [for myself], and the priest, and have gone away, and what more do I have? How then do you say to me, 'What's wrong with you?'"

Judges 19:8 LXX(H)
היום וַיֹּאכְלוּ [וַיִּשְׁתּוּ] שניהם: ויקם

Judges 19:8 And he arose early in the morning on the fifth day to depart; and the young lady's father said, "Please refresh yourself and stay until the day declines." And the two of them ate [and drank].

Judges 19:10 LXX(H) Mss
חבושים ופילגשו [ונערו] עמו: הם

Judges 19:10 But the man did not want to stay another night. He left and traveled as far as Jebus (that is, Jerusalem). He had with him a pair of saddled donkeys, and his concubine [and his servant] were with him.

Judges 19:28 LXX(H) (cf. PH)
ואין ענה [כי מתה] ויקחה על

Judges 19:28 And he said to her, "Get up, and let us go." But there was no answer, [for she was dead]. So he placed her on the donkey, and the man rose up, and went to his home.

Judges 19:30 LXX(H) Mss
מצרים עד היום הזה [ויצו האנשים אשר שלח לאמר כה תאמרו לכל־איש ישראל הנהיתה כדבר הזה למיום עלות בני־ ישראל מארץ מצרים עד היום הזה] שימו־לכם עליה עצו ודברו:

Judges 19:30 And it was so, that all who saw it said, "Nothing like this has been done or seen since the day that the children of Israel came up out of the land of Egypt until this day." [And he commanded the men whom he sent, saying, "This is what you will say to all the men of Israel, 'Has anything like this happened since the day that the children of Israel came up out of the land of Egypt until this day?] Consider it, take counsel, and speak.'"

Judges 20:9 LXX(H)
נעשה לגבעה [נעלה] עליה בגורל:

Judges 20:9 But now this is the thing which we will do to Gibeah: [we will go up] against it by lot;

Judges 20:10 LXX(H)
לעם [לבאים] לעשות לבואם לגבעה

Judges 20:10 and we will take ten men of one hundred throughout all the tribes of Israel, (and one hundred of one thousand, and a thousand out of ten thousand), to get food for the people, [those setting forth,] that when they come to Gibeah of Benjamin they may repay all the disgrace that they have committed in Israel."

Judges 20:18 LXX(H)
יְהוּדָה [יַעֲלֶה] בַּתְּחִלָּה: וַיָּקוּמוּ

Judges 20:18 The children of Israel arose, and went up to Bethel, and asked counsel of God; and they said, "Who shall go up for us first to battle against the children of Benjamin?" The LORD said, "Judah [will go up] first."

Judges 21:11 LXX(H)
תַחֲרִימוּ [וְאֶת הַבְּתוּלוֹת תְּחַיּוּ וַיַּעֲשׂוּ כֵן]: וַיִּמְצְאוּ

Judges 21:11 This is the thing that you shall do: you shall utterly destroy every male, and every woman who has slept with a man, [but the virgins you are to keep alive." And they did so.]

Ruth 1:14 LXX(H)
לַחֲמוֹתָהּ [וַתֵּשֶׁב אֶל עַמָּהּ] וְרוּת

Ruth 1:14 And they lifted up their voice, and wept again; and Orpah kissed her mother-in-law [and returned to her people], but Ruth clung to her.

Ruth 3:17 MT qere LXX (Syr) Tg
אָמַר [אֵלַי] אַל תָּבוֹאִי

Ruth 3:17 She said, "He gave me these six measures of barley; for he said [to me] 'Do not go empty-handed to your mother-in-law.'"

Ruth 4:8 LXX(H)
נַעֲלוֹ [וַיִּתֶּן לוֹ]: וַיֹּאמֶר

Ruth 4:8 So the near kinsman said to Boaz, "Buy it for yourself." And he took off his sandal [and gave it to him]. And said...

1Samuel 1:9 LXX(H)
שָׁתֹה [וַתִּתְיַצֵּב לִפְנֵי יְהוָה] וְעֵלִי

1 Samuel 1:9 So Hannah rose after eating and drinking in Shiloh [and stood before the LORD]. Now Eli the priest was sitting on the seat by the doorpost of the temple of the LORD.

1Samuel 1:18 LXX(H)
האשה לדרכה [ותבא הלשכתה] ותאכל

1 Samuel 1:18 She said, "Let your handmaid find favor in your sight." So the woman went her way [and entered her quarters] and ate; and her facial expression wasn't sad any more.

1Samuel 1:21 LXX(H) Mss OL
ואת נדרו [לשלם ואת כל מעשרות ארצו] והנה

1 Samuel 1:21 The husband, Elkanah, and all his household, went up to offer to the LORD the yearly sacrifice, and his vow [redeem, and all the tithes of his land].

1Samuel 1:24 (DSS) + LXX(H)
ותעל אותו שילה כאשר בפר משלש ולחם ואיפה אחת קמח ונבל יין ותבאהו בית יהוה והנער [עמם ויבאו לפני יהוה וישחט אביהו את הזבח כאשר יעשה מימים ימימה ליהוה ויבא את] הנער: וישחט

1 Samuel 1:24 And she went up with him to Shiloh with a three-year old bull, and bread, and one ephah of flour, and a skin of wine, and brought him to the house of the LORD in Shiloh. And the child [was with them. And they went before the LORD, and his father slaughtered the sacrifice, which he did annually to the LORD. And he brought the] child,

1Samuel 2:24 LXX(H) Mss (sight confusion)
אל בני [אל תעשון כן] כי לוא טובה השמעה
אשר אנכי שמע מעברים עם יהוה:

1 Samuel 2:24 No, my sons, [do not do this]. For it is not a good report that I hear the LORD's people spreading.

1Samuel 2:25 DSS LXX
אם [חטוא] יחטא איש לאיש

1 Samuel 2:25 If a man sins [gravely] against another, he can appeal to the LORD; but if a man sins against the LORD, who can intercede for him?" But, they did not listen to the voice of their father, because the LORD intended to kill them.

1Samuel 2:27 DSS LXX
בְּמִצְרַיִם [עֲבָדִים] לְבֵית

1 Samuel 2:27 A man of God came to Eli, and said, "Thus says the LORD, I plainly revealed myself to the house of your father, when they were [slaves] in Egypt to the house of Pharaoh.

1Samuel 2:28 LXX(H)
בְּנֵי יִשְׂרָאֵל [לַאֲכֹל] לָמָּה

1 Samuel 2:28 And I chose him out of all the tribes of Israel to be my priest, to go up to my altar, to burn incense, to wear an ephod before me. And I gave to the house of your father all the offerings by fire of the children of Israel [as food].

1Samuel 3:4 (DSS) LXX(H)
וַיִּקְרָא יְהוָה שְׁמוּאֵל [שְׁמוּאֵל] וַיֹּאמֶר הִנֵּנִי:

1 Samuel 3:4 that the LORD called, "Samuel. [Samuel.]" And he said, "Here I am."

1Samuel 3:15 LXX(H)
עַד הַבֹּקֶר [וַיִּשְׁכְּם בַּבֹּקֶר] וַיִּפְתַּח אֶת

1 Samuel 3:15 And Samuel lay there until the morning, [and in the morning he got up] and opened the doors of the house of the LORD. And Samuel was afraid to tell Eli the vision.

1Samuel 3:17 LXX(H)
דָּבָר אֵלֶיךָ [בְּאָזְנֶיךָ]: וַיַּגֶּד לוֹ

1 Samuel 3:17 And he said, "What is the thing that he has spoken to you? Please do not hide it from me. God do so to you, and more also, if you hide anything from me of all the things that he spoke to you [in your ears]."

1Samuel 4:1 LXX(H)
ויהי דבר שמואל לכל ישראל [ועלי זקן מאד ובניו הלכו והרע דרכם
לפני יהוה ועלי זקן מאד ובניו הלכו הלוך והרע דרכם לפני יהוה ויהי
בימים ההם ויקבצו פלש פלשתים למלחמה על ישראל] ויצא ישראל

1 Samuel 4:1 And Samuel's words came to all Israel. [And Eli grew very old, and his sons kept advancing in their wicked behavior before the LORD. And it came to pass in those days that the Philistines gathered themselves together against Israel.] And Israel went out against the Philistines to battle, and camped beside Ebenezer; and the Philistines camped in Aphek.

1Samuel 5:6 LXX(H) Mss
את אשדוד ואת גבולה [ויעל עליהם עכברים וישרצו בעניותם ובתך
ארצם עלו עכברים ותהי מהומת מות בעיר הגדולה] ויראו

1 Samuel 5:6 But the hand of the LORD was heavy upon the Ashdodites, and he ravaged them and afflicted them with tumors, both Ashdod and it's territory. [And he brought up against them mice, and they burst out in their ships, and mice sprang up in the midst of their land, and there was a great terror of death in the city.]

1Samuel 5:11 DSS LXX Mss (sight confusion)
כבדה מאד [כבוא אר]ון האלהים שמה

1 Samuel 5:11 And they sent and gathered together all the lords of the Philistines, and they said, "Send away the ark of the God of Israel, and let it go again to its own place, so that it will not kill us and our people." For there was a very heavy terror of death throughout all the city when [arrived the ark] of God there.

1Samuel 6:3 LXX(H)
משלחים [אתם] את ארון

1 Samuel 6:3 They said, "If you [are going to] send away the ark of the God of Israel, do not send it empty; but by all means return him a trespass offering: then you shall be healed, and it shall be known to you why his hand is not removed from you."

1Samuel 8:12 LXX(H)
וְלַקְצֹר קְצִירוֹ [וְלַבְצִיר בְּצִירוֹ] וְלַעֲשׂוֹת

1 Samuel 8:12 And he will appoint for himself commanders of thousands, and commanders of fifties; and he will assign some to plow his ground, and to reap his harvest, [and gather his vintage,] and to make his implements of war, and the equipment of his chariots.

1Samuel 9:3 LXX Mss Syr
בקש את האתנת [וַיָּקָם שאול ויקח את אחד מנערי אביו אתו וילך לבקש את אתנות קיש אביו] וַיַּעֲבֹר בהר

1 Samuel 9:3 Now the donkeys of Kish, Saul's father, were lost. And Kish said to Saul his son, "Take now one of the servants with you, and arise, go and look for the donkeys." [So Saul got up and took one of the servants of his father with him and went to look for the donkeys of his father Kish.]

1Samuel 9:16 LXX(H)
ראיתי את [עֳנִי] עַמִּי כי

1 Samuel 9:16 "Tomorrow about this time I will send you a man out of the land of Benjamin, and you shall anoint him to be prince over my people Israel; and he shall save my people out of the hand of the Philistines; for I have seen [the suffering of] my people, because their cry has come to me."

1Samuel 10:1 LXX(H)
ויאמר הלוא [מְשָׁחֲךָ יהוה לנגיד על עמו על ישראל ואתה תעצר בעם יהוה ואתה תושיענו מיד איביו מסביב וזה לך האות] כי מְשָׁחֲךָ יהוה על נחלתו לנגיד

1 Samuel 10:1 Then Samuel took the vial of oil and poured it on his head, and kissed him, and said, ["Has not the LORD anointed you to be ruler over his people Israel? And you shall rule over the people of the LORD, and you shall save them out of the hand of their enemies all around. And this shall be the sign to you] that the LORD has anointed you to be ruler over his inheritance.

1Samuel 10:21 LXX(H) OL

המטרי [וַיַּקְרֵב את משפחת מטרי לגברים] וַיִּלָּכֵד

1 Samuel 10:21 He brought the tribe of Benjamin near by their families, and the family of the Matrites was taken. [And he brought the family of the Matrites near man by man,] and Saul the son of Kish was taken. But when they looked for him, he could not be found.

1Samuel 10:27-11:1 DSS

לו מנחה [וְנָחָשׁ מלך בני עַמּוֹן הוא לחץ את בני גד ואת בני ראובן בחזקה ונקר להם כול עין ימין אין מושיע לישראל ולוא נשאר איש בבני ישראל אשר בעבר הירדן אשר לוא נקר לו נחש מלך בני עמון כול עין ימין והן שבאת אלפים איש נצלו מיד בני עמון ויבאו אל יבש גלעד] 11:1 ויהי כמו חדש] וַיַּעַל נָחָשׁ הָעַמּוֹנִי

1 Samuel 10:27-11:1a "But certain worthless fellows said, "How shall this man save us?" They despised him, and brought him no present. [Now Nahash, king of the Ammonites, was severely oppressing the Gadites and the Reubenites. He put out the right eye of all of them, and he would not allow anyone to rescue Israel. Not one was left of the children of Israel beyond the Jordan whose right eye Nahash, king of the Ammonites, did not put out, except for seven thousand men who had escaped from the Ammonites and went to Jabesh Gilead.11:1 After about a month,] Nahash the Ammonite came up and camped against Jabesh Gilead: and all the men of Jabesh said to Nahash, "Make a covenant with us, and we will serve you."

1Samuel 12:8 LXX(H)

יעקב מִצְרַיִם [וַיְעַנֵּם מִצְרַיִם] וַיִּזְעֲקוּ

1 Samuel 12:8 "When Jacob went into Egypt, [and the Egyptians oppressed them,] and your fathers cried to the LORD, then the LORD sent Moses and Aaron, who brought your fathers out of Egypt, and made them to dwell in this place.

1Samuel 12:14 LXX(H) Mss cf. DSS spacing

יהוה אלהיכֶם [וְהִצַּלְכֶם]: ואם

1 Samuel 12:14 If you will fear the LORD, and serve him, and listen to his voice, and not rebel against the commandment of the LORD, and both you and also the king who reigns over you are followers of the LORD your God, [then he will rescue you].

1Samuel 12:15 LXX Mss
יד יהוה בכם ובמלככם [לאבידכם]: גם עתה

1 Samuel 12:15 But if you will not listen to the voice of the LORD, but rebel against the commandment of the LORD, then the hand of the LORD will be against you and against your king [to destroy you].

1Samuel 13:5 LXX(H)
עם ישראל [ויעלו על ישראל] שלשים

1 Samuel 13:5 The Philistines assembled themselves together to fight with Israel, [and brought up against Israel] three thousand chariots, and six thousand horsemen, and people as the sand which is on the seashore in multitude: and they came up, and camped in Michmash, eastward of Beth Aven.

1Samuel 13:15 LXX(H)
ויקם שמואל ויעל מן הגלגל [לדרכו ויתר העם עלה אחרי שאול לקראת עם המלחמה ויבאו מן הגלגל] גבעת בנימן ויפקד שאול את העם הנמצאים עמו כשש מאות איש

1 Samuel 13:15 And Samuel arose and departed from Gilgal, [and the rest of the people went up after Saul to meet him after the men of war, when they had come up from Gilgal] to Gibeah of Benjamin. And Saul numbered the people who were present with him, about six hundred men.

1Samuel 14:16 LXX(H)
נמוג וילך [הלם] והלם: ויאמר

1 Samuel 14:16 And the watchmen of Saul in Gibeah of Benjamin looked, and behold, the multitude was scattering [here] and there.

1Samuel 14:41 LXX(H)
אלהי ישראל [למה לא ענת את עבדך היום אם יש בי אי ביונתן בני העון הזה יהוה אלהי ישראל הבה יורים ואם ישנו בעמך ישראל] הבה תמים

1 Samuel 14:41 Therefore Saul said, "LORD, God of Israel, [why have you not answered your servant this day? If this sin is mine or in Jonathan my son, LORD, God of Israel, give Urim. But if this sin is in your people Israel,] give Thummim." And Jonathan and Saul were chosen, but the people were cleared.

1Samuel 14:42 LXX(H)

ויאמר שאול הפילו <u>ביני ובין יונתן בני</u> [את אשר ילכד
והוה ימות ויאמר העם אל שאול לא יהיה כדבר הזה ויחזק
שאול בעם ויפילו <u>בינו ובין יונתן בנו</u>] וילכד יונתן

1 Samuel 14:42 And Saul said, "Cast lots between me and Jonathan my son. [Whomever the LORD shall indicate to be taken by lot, let him die." And the people said to Saul, "This thing is not to be." And Saul prevailed over the people, and they cast lots between him and Jonathan his son.] And Jonathan was selected.

1 Samuel 15:12-13 LXX(H) Mss

וירד הגלגל [<u>ויבא שמואל אל שאול</u> והנה היא העלה עלות ליהוה
את ראשית השלל אשר לקח מעמלק] <u>ויבא שמואל אל שאול</u>

1 Samuel 15:12 And Samuel rose early to meet Saul in the morning; and it was told Samuel, saying, "Saul came to Carmel, and behold, he set up a monument for himself, and turned, and passed on, and went down to Gilgal" [And Samuel came to Saul, and behold, he was offering up a burnt offering to the LORD, the best of the spoils which he had brought from Amalek.] 13 And Samuel came to Saul;

1 Samuel 16:7 LXX(H)

האדם [<u>יראה האלהים</u>] יראה לעינים

1 Samuel 16:7 But the LORD said to Samuel, "Do not look on his face, or on the height of his stature; because I have rejected him. For man does not [see as God] sees, for man looks at the outward appearance, but the LORD looks at the heart."

1 Samuel 16:16 LXX(H)

וטוב <u>לך</u> [<u>והניחה לך</u>]: <u>ויאמר</u>

1 Samuel 16:16 Let our lord now command your servants who are before you, to seek out a man who is a skillful player on the harp. It will happen, when the evil spirit from God is on you, that he will play with his hand, and you will be well, [and it will give you relief]."

1 Samuel 16:20 LXX(H) Mss OL

ויקח ישי ח<u>מור</u> [וישם עליו <u>עמר</u>] לחם ונאד

1 Samuel 16:20 And Jesse took a donkey [and loaded it with an omer of] bread, and a skin of wine, and a young goat, and sent them by David his son to Saul.

1 Samuel 17:36 LXX(H) (MT partially repaired ())

הפלשתי הערל הזה [(כאחד מהם) הלוא אלך והכתיו והסירתי היום חרף מישראל כי מי הערל הזה] כי חרף מערכת

1 Samuel 17:36 Your servant struck both the lion and the bear, and this uncircumcised Philistine [(shall be as one of them.) Should I not go and smite him, and remove this day a reproach from Israel? For who is this uncircumcised one,] since he has defied the armies of the living God?"

1 Samuel 19:22 LXX(H)

גם המה: [ויחר אף שאול] וילך גם הוא הרמתה ויבא עד־בור [הגרן] אשר [בשפי] וישאל ויאמר איפה שמואל ודוד ויאמר הנה בנוית ברמה:

1 Samuel 19:22 [And Saul became very angry,] and he himself went to Ramah, and came to the cistern of the threshing floor that is on the bare hill. And he asked, "Where are Samuel and David?" And one said, "Behold, they are at Naioth in Ramah."

1Samuel 21:4 DSS

הנערים מאשה [ואכלתם ממנו]: ויען

1 Samuel 21:4 The priest answered David, and said, "There is no common bread under my hand, but there is holy bread. If the young men have kept themselves from women, [they may eat of it]."

1Samuel 23:6 LXX(H) Mss

אל דוד [והוא את דוד] קעילה

1 Samuel 23:6 It happened, when Abiathar the son of Ahimelech fled to David, [that he with David] went down to Keilah, having an ephod in his hand.

1Samuel 24:10 Vg(H)

ותחס [עיני] עליך ואמר

1 Samuel 24:10 Behold, this day your eyes have seen how that the LORD had delivered you today into my hand in the cave. Some urged me to kill you, but [my eye] spared you; and I said, 'I will not put forth my hand against my lord; for he is the LORD's anointed.'

1Samuel 25:7 LXX(H)
ועתה [הנה] שמעתי

1 Samuel 25:7 And now, [behold,] I have heard that you have shearers. Now your shepherds have been with us in the wilderness, and we did not hurt them, neither was there anything missing from them, all the while they were in Carmel.

1Samuel 25:11 LXX(H) OL Mss
טבחתי לגזזי [צאני] ונתתי

1 Samuel 25:11 Shall I then take my bread, and my wine, and my meat that I have slaughtered for the shearers [of my sheep], and give it to men who I do not know where they come from?"

1Samuel 29:10 LXX(H) OL Mss
באו אתך [והלכתם אל המקום אשר הפקדתי אתכם שם ודבר בליעל אל תשם בלבבך כי טוב אתה לפני והשכמתם בדרך] והשכמתם בבקר

1 Samuel 29:10 Therefore now rise up early in the morning, you and the servants of your lord who have come with you, [and go to the place which I allotted to you. As for evil remarks, take none to heart; for you are good in my sight.] And as soon as you are up early in the morning, and have light, depart."

1Samuel 30:15 LXX(H) Mss
אל הגדוד הזה [וישבע לון]: וירדהו

1 Samuel 30:15 And David said to him, "Will you bring me down to this troop?" And he said, "Swear to me by God that you will neither kill me, nor deliver me up into the hands of my master, and I will bring you down to this troop." [And he swore to him.] 16 And when he brought him down...

1Samuel 30:17 LXX(H) Mss
הערב למחרתם [וימיתם] ולא נמלט

1 Samuel 30:17 And David struck them from the twilight even to the evening of the next day [and he put them to death]. Not a man of them escaped from there, except four hundred young men who rode on camels and fled.

2Samuel 1:23 LXX(H)

שאול ויהונתן הנאהבים והנ<u>עימם</u> [לא נבדלים <u>נעימם</u>]
בחייהם ובמותם לא נפרדו מנשרים קלו מאריות גברו:

2 Samuel 1:23 Saul and Jonathan, beloved and lovely, [not separated. Lovely] in their life, and in their death they were not separated. They were swifter than eagles. They were stronger than lions.

2Samuel 3:8 LXX(H) Mss

ליהודה [<u>הלי</u>] <u>היום אעשה</u> [את כל אלה ו<u>אעשה</u>] חסד

2 Samuel 3:8 Then Abner was very angry over the words of Ishbosheth, and said, "Am I a dog's head that belongs to Judah? Until today, [is it for myself] that I have been doing [all these things, and showing] loyalty to the house of Saul your father, to his brothers, and to his friends, and have not delivered you into the hand of David? And yet you charge me this day with a fault concerning this woman.

2Samuel 6:9 LXX(H) Mss

וירא דוד את יהוה ביום ההוא ויאמר איך יבוא
אלי <u>ארון</u> [האלהים ויבא <u>ארון</u>] יהוה

2 Samuel 6:9 And David was afraid of the LORD that day; and he said, "How can come to me the ark of [God?" Now arrived the ark of] the LORD,

2Samuel 6:12 LXX(H) OL

ויגד למלך דוד לאמר ברך יהוה את בית עבד אדם ואת כל אשר
לו בעבור ארון האלהים [<u>ויאמר דוד</u> אשיב את הברכה אל ביתי]
<u>וילך דוד</u> ויעל את ארון יהוה מבית עבד אדם עיר דוד בשמחה

2 Samuel 6:12 And it was told king David, saying, "The LORD has blessed the house of Obed-Edom and all that belongs to him because of the ark of God." [And David said, "I will bring back the blessing to my house."] And David went and brought up the ark of the LORD from the house of Obed-Edom into the City of David with joy.

2 Samuel 6:21a LXX(H) Mss
ויאמר דוד אל מיכל לפני יהוה [ארקד ברוך יהוה] אשר

2 Samuel 6:21 And David said to Michal, "Before the LORD [I was dancing. Blessed be the LORD,] who chose me above your father, and above all his house, to appoint me prince over the people of the LORD, over Israel; therefore I will celebrate before the LORD.

2 Samuel 8:7 OL(H) cf. (DSS) LXX
ויביאם ירושלם [גם אתם לקח אחר שישק מלך מצרים בימי רחבעם בן שלמה בעלתו אל ירושלם]: ומטבח

2 Samuel 8:7 And David took the shields of gold that were on the servants of Hadadezer, and brought them to Jerusalem, [which, later on, were also taken by Shishak king of Egypt in the days of Rehoboam son of Solomon, when he went up to Jerusalem].

2 Samuel 11:7 LXX(H) Mss cf. OL
ולשלום המלחמה [ויאמר לשלום]: ויאמר דוד

2 Samuel 11:7 When Uriah had come to him, David asked of him how Joab did, and how the people fared, and how the war was going. [And he said, "Well."] 8 And said David...

2Samuel 13:21-22 DSS LXX
מאד [ולא עצב את רוח אמנון בנו כי אהבו כי בכורו הוא]: ולא דבר

2 Samuel 13:21 But when king David heard of all these things, he was very angry. [But he did not inflict pain on the spirit of his son Amnon, because he loved him, for he was his firstborn.]

2Samuel 13:27 (DSS) LXX(H)
כל בני המלך [ויעש אבשלום משתה כמשתה המלך]

2 Samuel 13:27 But Absalom pressed him, and he let Amnon and all the king's sons go with him. [And Absalom prepared a feast like a king's feast.]

(2 Samuel 6 with restorations)

2 Samuel

6 And David again gathered together all the chosen men of Israel, thirty thousand. ²And David arose, and went with all the people who were with him, from Baale Judah, to bring up from there the ark of God, which is called there by the name of the LORD of hosts who sits above the cherubim.

³And they set the ark of God on a new cart, and brought it out of the house of Abinadab that was on the hill. And Uzzah and Ahio, the sons of Abinadab, were guiding the cart ⁴with the ark of God; and Uzzah and Ahio were walking in front of and by the side of the ark. ⁵And David and all the children of Israel played before the LORD with all their strength and with songs, and with harps, and with stringed instruments, and with tambourines, and with castanets, and with cymbals.

⁶And when they came to the threshing floor of Nacon, Uzzah reached out his hand to the ark of God, and took hold of it; for the cattle stumbled. ⁷And the anger of the LORD was kindled against Uzzah; and God struck him there for his error; and there he died by the ark of God.

⁸And David was displeased, because the LORD had broken forth on Uzzah; and he called that place Perez Uzzah, to this day. ⁹And David was afraid of the LORD that day; and he said, "How can the ark of God come to me?" Now the ark of the LORD arrived, ¹⁰but David was not willing to move the ark of the LORD with him to the City of David; so David diverted it to the house of Obed-Edom the Gittite.

¹¹And the ark of the LORD remained in the house of Obed-Edom the Gittite three months, and the LORD blessed Obed-Edom and all his house. ¹²And it was told king David, saying, "The LORD has blessed the house of Obed-Edom and all that belongs to him because of the ark of God." And David said, "I will bring back the blessing to my house." And David went and brought up the ark of the LORD from the house of Obed-Edom into the City of David with joy.

¹³And it was so, that, when those who bore the ark of the LORD had gone six steps, he sacrificed an ox and a fattened calf. ¹⁴And David danced before the LORD with all his might; and David was clothed in a linen ephod.

¹⁵So David and all the house of Israel brought up the ark of the LORD with shouting, and with the sound of the trumpet. ¹⁶And it was so, as the ark of the LORD came into the City of David, that Michal the daughter of Saul looked out at the window, and saw king David leaping and dancing before the LORD; and she despised him in her heart.

¹⁷And they brought in the ark of the LORD, and set it in its place, in the midst of the tent that David had set up for it; and David offered burnt offerings and peace offerings before the LORD. ¹⁸And when David had made an end of offering the burnt offering and the peace offerings, he blessed the people in the name of the LORD of hosts.

¹⁹And he gave to all the people, even among the whole multitude of Israel, both to men and women, to everyone a portion of bread, a date cake, and a raisin cake. So all the people departed everyone to his house.

²⁰Then David returned to bless his household. And Michal the daughter of Saul came out to meet David, and said, "How glorious the king of Israel was today, who uncovered himself today in the eyes of the handmaids of his servants, as one of the vain fellows shamelessly uncovers himself."

²¹And David said to Michal, "I was dancing before the LORD. Blessed be the LORD, who chose me above your father, and above all his house, to appoint me prince over the people of the LORD, over Israel; therefore I will celebrate before the LORD. ²²And I will be yet more vile than this, and will be lowly in your eyes. But of the handmaids of whom you have spoken, they shall honor me." ²³And Michal the daughter of Saul had no child to the day of her death.

2Samuel 13:34 LXX(H)
אחריו <u>מצד ההר</u> [בדרך חרנים מצד ההר במורד ויבא הצפה ויגד למלך ויאמר אנשים ראיתי מדרך חרנים <u>מצד ההר</u>]: ויאמר

2 Samuel 13:34 But Absalom fled. And the young man who kept the watch lifted up his eyes, and looked, and behold, many men were coming on the road behind him from the side of the mountain [in the descent. And the watchman came and told the king, and said, "I have seen many men coming from the Horonaim road by the side of the mountain."]

2Samuel 14:30 DSS LXX OL
עבדי אבשלום את החלקה באש [ויבואו ילדי יואב אלו קרועי בגדיהם ויאומרו הציתו אבדי אבשלום את החלקה באש]

2 Samuel 14:30 Therefore he said to his servants, "Behold, Joab's field is near mine, and he has barley there. Go and set it on fire." Absalom's servants set the field on fire. [And the servants of Joab came to him with their clothes rent, and they said to him, "The servants of Absalom have set the field on fire.]"

2Samuel 15:20 LXX(H)
את אחיך עִמָּךְ [ויהוה יעשה עִמָּךְ] חסד ואמת

2 Samuel 15:20 You came only yesterday. Should I today make you wander about with us, since I go I know not where? Go back, and take your brothers with you, [and may the LORD show you] kindness and truth."

2Samuel 15:34 LXX(H)
לאבשלום [עָבְרוּ אחיך והמלך אחרי עבר אביך ועתה] עַבְדְּךָ אני

2 Samuel 15:34 but if you return to the city, and tell Absalom, '[Your brothers have left, O king, after your father left, and now] I will be your servant, O king. As I have been your father's servant in time past, so now I will be your servant,' then you will defeat for me the counsel of Ahithophel.

2Samuel 16:14 LXX(H) Ms
אשר אתו [על הירדן] עֵיפִים וינפש שם

2Samuel 16:14 The king, and all the people who were with him, arrived weary [at the Jordan,] and he refreshed himself there.

2Samuel 17:11 LXX(H)
כִּי [כה יעץ אנֹכִי] יעצתי

2 Samuel 17:11 But, [I as follows strongly] advise, that all Israel be gathered together to you, from Dan even to Beersheba, as the sand that is by the sea for multitude; and that you personally go into battle.

2Samuel 18:23 LXX(H) Syr Vg
מצאת: [וַיֹּאמֶר] וַיְהִי מה ארוץ ויאמר

2Samuel 18:23 [And he said,] "But come what may, I will run." And he said to him, "Run." Then Ahimaaz ran by the way of the Plain, and outran the Cushite.

2Samuel 18:24 LXX(H)
איש רץ לַבַדּוֹ [לְפָנָיו]: ויקרא

2 Samuel 18:24 Now David was sitting between the two gates, and the watchman went up to the roof of the gate to the wall and lifted up his eyes and looked. And behold, a man was running alone [towards him].

2Samuel 19:10 LXX(H) OL (MT restored in v.11)
להשיב את <u>המלך</u> [ודבר כל ישראל בא אל <u>המלך</u>]: <u>והמלך</u> דוד

2 Samuel 19:10 Absalom, whom we anointed over us, has died in battle. Now therefore why do you not speak a word of bringing the king back?" [And the talk of all Israel came to the king.] 11 So king David sent to Zadok and to Abiathar the priests, saying, "Speak to the elders of Judah, saying, 'Why are you the last to bring the king back to his house?

2Samuel 24:15 LXX(H)
מועד [<u>ויחל</u> המכה בעם] <u>וימת</u>

2 Samuel 24:15 So the LORD sent a pestilence on Israel from the morning even to the appointed time; [and the destruction began among the people.] And there died of the people from Dan even to Beersheba seventy thousand men.

2Samuel 24:16 DSS
ארנה היבסי [<u>וישא דויד את</u> עיניו וירא את מלאך יהוה עומד בין הארץ ובין השמים וחרבו שלופה בידו נטואה על ירושלים ויפלו הזקנים על פניהם מתכסים בשקים]: <u>ויאמר דויד אל</u>

2 Samuel 24:16 When the angel stretched out his hand toward Jerusalem to destroy it, the LORD relented of the disaster, and said to the angel who destroyed the people, "It is enough. Now stay your hand." The angel of the LORD was by the threshing floor of Araunah the Jebusite. [And David lifted up his eyes and saw the angel of the LORD standing between earth and the sky, having a drawn sword in his hand stretched out over Jerusalem. Then David and the elders, clothed in sackcloth, fell down on their faces.] 17 And David spoke...

2Samuel 24:17 DSS LXX Mss
חטאתי ואנכי [<u>הרעה</u>] <u>הרעתי</u> ואלה

2Samuel 24:17 And David spoke to the LORD when he saw the angel who struck the people, and said, "Behold, I have sinned, and I, [the shepherd,] have done great evil. But these sheep, what have they done? Please let your hand be against me, and against my father's house."

1Kings 2:13 LXX(H)
אם שלמה [וישתחו לה] ותאמר השלום

1Kings 2:13 Then Adonijah the son of Haggith came to Bathsheba the mother of Solomon, [and did homage to her]. And she said, "Do you come peaceably?" And he said, "Peaceably."

1Kings 2:29 LXX(H)
המזבח וישלח שלמה את [יואב לאמר מה היה לך כי נסת אל המזבח ויאמר יואב כי ירא אני יראתי מפניך ואנס אל יהוה וישלח שלמה את] בניהו בן יהוידע לאמר לך פגע בו

1 Kings 2:29 It was told king Solomon, "Joab has fled to the Tent of the LORD, and behold, he is by the altar." And Solomon sent to [Joab, saying, "What happened to you, that you have fled to the altar?" And Joab said, "Because I was afraid of you, so I fled to the LORD." And Solomon sent to] Benaiah the son of Jehoiada, saying, "Go, fall on him."

1Kings 3:15 LXX(H)
שלמה חלום [ויקם] ויבוא ירושלם

1 Kings 3:15 And Solomon awoke, and behold, it was a dream. [And he arose] and came to Jerusalem, and stood before the ark of the covenant of the LORD, and offered up burnt offerings, offered peace offerings, and made a feast for all his servants.

1Kings 4:19 LXX(H)
אחד אשר בארץ [יהודה]: יהודה וישראל רבים

1 Kings 4:19 Geber the son of Uri, in the land of Gilead, the country of Sihon king of the Amorites and of Og king of Bashan; and he was the only prefect in the land of [Judah]. 20 Judah and Israel were...

1Kings 5:11(25) LXX(H)
כר חטים מכלת לביתו ועשרים [אלף בתים] שמן כתית

1 Kings 5:11 Solomon gave Hiram twenty thousand cors of wheat for food to his household, and twenty [thousand baths] of pure oil. Solomon gave this to Hiram year by year.

1Kings 7:3 LXX(H)
על העמודים [ומספר העמודים] ארבעים

1 Kings 7:3 It was covered with cedar above atop the beams which were on the pillars, [and the pillars numbered] forty-five; fifteen in a row.

1Kings 7:15 Syr(H) Tg LXX Mss
וסב את [העמוד האחד ועביו ארבע אצבעות נבוב וכן] העמוד השני

1 Kings 7:15 For he cast the two pillars of bronze, eighteen cubits was the height of one pillar; and a line of twelve cubits could encompass [the one pillar, and its thickness hollowed out was four fingers; and so was] the second pillar.

1Kings 7:20 Syr(H)
סביב על [הכתרת האחת וכן על] הכתרת השנית

1 Kings 7:20 And the capitals were on the two pillars, even above and close to the rounded projection which was beside the network. And there were two hundred pomegranates in rows all around on [the capital, and the same around] the other capital

1Kings 8:16 DSS+LXX(H)
לבנות בית להיות שמי שם [ולא בחרתי באיש להיות נגיד על עי ישראל ואבחר בירושלם להיות שמי שם] ואבחר בדוד להיות על עמי ישראל

1 Kings 8:16 'Since the day that I brought my people Israel out of Egypt, I chose no city out of all the tribes of Israel to build a house, that my name might be there, [nor did I choose any man to be a leader over my people Israel; but I chose Jerusalem that my name may be there,] and I chose David to be over my people Israel.'

1 Kings 8:52 LXX(H)
להיות עיניך [ואזניך] פתחות אל תחנת

1 Kings 8:52 that your eyes [and your ears] may be open to the petition of your servant, and to the petition of your people Israel, to listen to them whenever they cry to you.

1Kings 8:65 LXX(H)

מצרים לפני יהוה אלהינו [בבית אשר בנה אכל ושתה ושמח לפני יהוה אלהינו]　שבעת ימים ושבעת ימים ארבעה עשר יום: ביום השמיני

1 Kings 8:65 So Solomon held the feast at that time, and all Israel with him, a great assembly, from Lebo Hamath to the Wadi of Egypt, before the LORD our God [in the house which he built, eating and drinking and rejoicing before the LORD our God,] seven days and seven days; fourteen days.

1Kings 8:65 LXX Mss > LXX

κυριου θεου ημων επτα ημεπασ [και επτα ημεπασ τεσσαρασ και δεκα ημεπασ] και εν τη ημερα

1 Kings 8:65 So Solomon held the feast at that time, and all Israel with him, a great assembly, from Lebo Hamath to the Wadi of Egypt, before the LORD our God in the house which he built, eating and drinking and rejoicing before the LORD our God, seven days [and seven days; fourteen days]. 66 And on the eighth day

1 Kings 9:3 LXX(H)

התחננתה לפני [עשיתי לך ככל תפלתך] הקדשתי את הבית

1 Kings 9:3 And the LORD said to him, "I have heard your prayer and your petition that you have made before me. [I have done for you according to all your prayer.] I have consecrated this house which you have built, to place my name there forever, and my eyes and my heart will be there perpetually.

1 Kings 11:1 LXX(H)

והמלך שלמה אהב נשים [ויקח נשים] נכריות רבות

1 Kings 11:1 Now king Solomon loved women, [and he took women] many foreign, together with the daughter of Pharaoh, women of the Moabites, Ammonites, Edomites, Sidonians, and Hittites;

1Kings 11:29 LXX(H)

אחיה השילני הנביא בדרך [ויסירהו מן הדרך] והוא

1 Kings 11:29 And it happened at that time, when Jeroboam went out of Jerusalem, that the prophet Ahijah the Shilonite found him on the way [and caused him to turn aside out of the way]. Now he had dressed himself with a new garment, and the two were alone in the countryside.

1Kings 12:2 LXX(H)
במצרים [שלח ויבא לעירו לארץ צררה אשר בחר אפרים] וישלחו

1 Kings 12:2 And it happened, when Jeroboam the son of Nebat heard of it (for he was still in Egypt, where he had fled from the presence of king Solomon, and Jeroboam lived in Egypt), [he came straight to his own city in the land of Zererah in the hill country of Ephraim] 3 And they sent....

1Kings 12:30 LXX(H)
העם לפני האחד [בית אל ולפני האחד] עד דן

1 Kings 12:30 Then this thing became a sin, for the people went before the one [at Bethel and before the one] as far as Dan.

1Kings 16:22 LXX(H)
תבני [וירם אחיו בעת ההיא] וימלך עמרי [אחרי תבני]: בשנת

1 Kings 16:22 But the people who followed Omri prevailed against the people who followed Tibni the son of Ginath. So Tibni died [and Joram his brother at that time], and Omri became king [in the place of Tibni].

1Kings 18:22-23 LXX(H)
וחמשים איש [ונביאי האשרה ארבע מאות]: ויתנו

1 Kings 18:22 Then Elijah said to the people, "I, even I only, am left a prophet of the LORD; but the prophets of Baal are four hundred and fifty men, [and the prophets of Asherah four hundred].

1Kings 18:43 LXX(H)
שב שבע פעמים [וישב הנער שבע פעמים]: ויהי

1 Kings 18:43 And he said to his servant, "Go up now, look toward the sea." So he went up, and looked, and said, "There is nothing." Then he said, "Go again" seven times. [And the servant went again seven times.]

1Kings 21:21 LXX(H) Mss
בעיני יהוה [להכעיסו: כה אמר יהוה] הנני

1 Kings 21:20 And Ahab said to Elijah, "Have you found me, my enemy?" And he answered, "I have found you, because you have sold yourself to do that which is evil in the sight of the LORD, [to provoke him to anger. 21 Thus says the LORD,] Behold, I will bring disaster on you, and will utterly sweep you away and will cut off from Ahab everyone, slave or free in Israel.

2Kings 1:17 LXX(H) Mss Syr Vg
יהורם [אחיו] תחתיו בשנת

2 Kings 1:17 So he died according to the word of the LORD which Elijah had spoken. And [his brother] Jehoram began to reign in his place in the second year of Jehoram the son of Jehoshaphat king of Judah; because he had no son.

2Kings 2:14 LXX(H) Mss (cf. early square script)
את המים [ולא יחצן] ויאמר איה יהוה אלהי אליהו אף הוא ויכה את המים [שנית] ויחצו הנה

2 Kings 2:14 He took the mantle of Elijah that fell from him, and struck the water, [and it did not divide]. And he said, "Where is the LORD, the God of Elijah, even he?" And he struck the water [a second time], and they divided to the one side and to the other; and Elisha crossed over.

2Kings 2:16 LXX(H) OL
רוח יהוה וישלכהו [בירדן או] באחד ההרים או

2 Kings 2:16 And they said to him, "See now, there are with your servants fifty strong men. Please let them go and seek your master. Perhaps the Spirit of the LORD has taken him up and thrown him [into the Jordan, or] on some mountain, or into some valley." And he said, "Do not send them."

2Kings 3:12 Hebrew Mss LXX Syr Vg
ויהושפט [מלך יהודה] ומלך אדום

2 Kings 3:12 And Jehoshaphat said, "The word of the LORD is with him." So the king of Israel and Jehoshaphat [king of Judah] and the king of Edom went down to him.

2Kings 5:12 LXX(H)
ישראל הלא [הלוך] ארחץ בהם

2 Kings 5:12 Aren't Abanah and Pharpar, the rivers of Damascus, better than all the waters of Israel? Couldn't I [go] wash in them, and be clean?" So he turned and went away in a rage.

2Kings 5:13 LXX(H) Mss Syr Tg Vg
ויאמרו אבי [אם] דבר גדול

2 Kings 5:13 His servants came near, and spoke to him, and said, "My father, [if] the prophet had asked you to do some great thing, wouldn't you have done it? How much rather then, when he says to you, 'Wash, and be clean?'"

2Kings 9:25 LXX(H) Syr
כי זכר [אני כי] אני ואתה

2 Kings 9:25 ...(Lit.:) "for remember [I when] I and you rode together" = "for I remember when you and I rode together"

2Kings 9:27 Syr(H) Vg Mss
הכהו [ויכהו] אל המרכבה

2 Kings 9:27 But when Ahaziah the king of Judah saw this, he fled by the way of the garden house. Jehu followed after him, and said, "Shoot him also." [And they shot him] in the chariot at the ascent of Gur, which is by Ibleam. He fled to Megiddo, and died there.

2Kings 10:15 Syr(H) cf. LXX Vg
יש [ויאמר] ויש

2 Kings 10:15 When he had departed from there, he met Jehonadab the son of Rechab coming to meet him. He greeted him, and said to him, "Is your heart right, as my heart is with your heart?" Jehonadab answered, "It is." [And he said], "If it is, give me your hand." He gave him his hand; and he took him up to him into the chariot.

2Kings 17:32 LXX(H)
ספרוים: [ויהיו יראים את יהוה ויעמידו תועבתם בבית הבמות אשר עשו בשמרון גוי גוי בעיר אשר הם ישבים שם] ויהיו יראים את יהוה ויעשו

2 Kings 17:32 [And they worshiped the LORD, yet they established their abominations in the houses of the high places which they made in Samaria, each nation in the city in which they dwelt.] And they worshiped the LORD, yet appointed from among themselves priests of the high places, who sacrificed for them in the houses of the high places.

2Kings 23:16 LXX(H)
קרא איש האלהים [בעמד ירבעם בחג על־המזבח ויפן וישא את־עיניו על קבר איש האלהים] אשר קרא

2 Kings 23:16 And as Josiah turned himself, he saw the tombs that were there in the mountain. And he sent, and took the bones out of the tombs, and burned them on the altar, and defiled it, according to the word of the LORD which the man of God [proclaimed, when Jeroboam stood by the altar at the feast. And he turned and raised his eyes to the tomb of the man of God] who proclaimed these things.

1Chronicles 1:4 LXX(H)
למך: נח [בני נח] שם חם ויפת

1 Chronicles 1:4 Noah. [The sons of Noah]: Shem, Ham, and Japheth.

1Chronicles 1:17 Hebrew Ms LXX
וארם [ובני ארם] ועוץ

1 Chronicles 1:17 The sons of Shem: Elam, and Asshur, and Arpachshad, and Lud, and Aram. [And the sons of Aram]: Uz, and Hul, and Gether, and Mash.

1Chronicles 6:15 (5:41) Tg(H)
ויהוצדק הלך [בגולה] בהגלות

1 Chronicles 6:15 And Jehozadak went [into captivity], when the LORD carried away Judah and Jerusalem by the hand of Nebuchadnezzar.

1Chronicles 6:27(12) LXX(H) Mss
אלקנה בְּנֵי [שמואל בְּנוֹ]: ובני

1 Chronicles 6:27 Eliab his son, Jeroham his son, Elkanah his son, [Samuel his son.]

1Chronicles 6:59(44) Syr(H) LXX Ms
ואת עשן ואת מגרשיה [ואת יטה ואת מגרשיה] ואת בית שמש

1 Chronicles 6:59 and Ashan with its suburbs, [and Juttah with its suburbs,] and Beth Shemesh with its suburbs;

1Chronicles 8:24 LXX(H)
וחנניה [וְעָמְרִי] וְעֵילָם וענתתיה:

1 Chronicles 8:24 and Hananiah, [and Omri,] and Elam, and Anthothijah,

1Chronicles 8:30 LXX(H)
ובנו הבכור עבדון וצור וקיש ובעל [וְנֵר] וְנָדָב:

1 Chronicles 8:30 and his firstborn son Abdon, and Zur, and Kish, and Baal, [and Ner,] and Nadab,

1Chronicles 8:31 LXX(H)
ואחיו וזכר [וּמִקְלוֹת]: וּמִקְלוֹת הוליד

1 Chronicles 8:31 and Gedor, and Ahio, and Zecher [and Mikloth]. 32 And Mikloth became...

1Chronicles 17:19 LXX(H)
להדיע [אֶת עבדך] אֶת כל הגדלות:

1 Chronicles 17:19 LORD, for your servant's sake, and according to your own heart, you have worked all this greatness, to make known [to your servant] all these great things.

1Chronicles 21:26 LXX(H)
מזבח העלה [ותאכל את העלה]: ויאמר

1 Chronicles 21:26 David built an altar to the LORD there, and offered burnt offerings and peace offerings, and called on the LORD; and he answered him from heaven by fire on the altar of burnt offering, [and it consumed the burnt offering.]

2Chronicles 12:16 LXX(H)
רחבעם עם אבתיו [ויקבר עם אבתיו] ויקבר בעיר דויד

2 Chronicles 12:16 And Rehoboam slept with his fathers, [and was buried with his fathers,] and was buried in the City of David. And Abijah his son reigned in his place.

2Chronicles 16:14 Tg(H) Vg
וזנים [מְרָקָחִים] מְרָקָחִים במרקחת

2 Chronicles 16:14 They buried him in his own tomb that he had dug out in the City of David, and laid him in the bed which was filled with spices and various kinds of [sweet-scented herbs] prepared by the perfumers' art, and they made a very great fire for him.

2Chronicles 23:3 LXX(H)
עם המלך [וירא אתם את בן המלך] ויאמר

2 Chronicles 23:3 All the assembly made a covenant in the house of God with the king. [And he showed them the son of the king.] And he said to them, "Behold, the son of the king shall reign, as the LORD has spoken concerning the sons of David.

2Chronicles 23:18 LXX(H)
ביד הכהנים והלוים [ויעמד את מחלקות הכהנים והלוים] אשר

2 Chronicles 23:18 Jehoiada appointed the officers of the house of the LORD under the hand of the priests and the Levites, [and he appointed the divisions of the priests and the Levites,] whom David had assigned over the house of the LORD, to offer the burnt offerings of the LORD, as it is written in the law of Moses, with rejoicing and with singing, according to the order of David.

2Chronicles 36:1 LXX(H)
בן יאשיהו [וימשחו אתו] וַיַמְלִיכהו

2 Chronicles 36:1 Then the people of the land took Jehoahaz the son of Josiah, [and they anointed him] and made him king in his father's place in Jerusalem.

Psalm 1:4 LXX(H)
תדפנו רוח [מֵעַל פני האדמה]: עַל כן

Psalm 1:4 Not so with the wicked, not so; instead, they are like the chaff which the wind drives away [from the surface of the ground].

Psalm 4:7(8) DSS LXX Syr
נתתה שמחה בלבי מעת דגנם ותירושם [וְיִצְהָרָם] רבו:

Psalm 4:7 You have put gladness in my heart, more than when their grain and wine [and oil] abound.

Psalm 11:4 LXX(H) Vg
יחזו [עַל דל] עַפְעַפָּיו

Psalm 11:4 The LORD is in his holy temple. The LORD is on his throne in heaven. His eyes look [upon the poor]. His eyes examine the children of men.

Psalm 13:6 LXX(H)
גמל עָלָי [ואזמרה שם יהוה עֶלְיוֹן]: למנצח

Psalm 13:6 I will sing to the LORD, because he has been good to me, [and I will sing to the name of the LORD Most High.]

Psalm 19:14 LXX(H) (sight confusion)
לפניך [תָּמִיד] יהוה

Psalm 19:14 Let the words of my mouth and the meditation of my heart be acceptable in your sight [always], LORD, my rock, and my redeemer.

Psalm 22:16 LXX(H) Aquila Symmachus Tg
כי סבבוני כלָבִים [רַבִּים] עדת מרעים הקיפוני כארו ידי ורגלי:

Psalm 22:16 For [many] dogs have surrounded me. A company of evildoers have enclosed me. They have pierced my hands and my feet.

Psalm 35:25 LXX(H)
בלבם [הָאָח] הָאָח נפשנו

Psalm 35:25 Do not let them say in their heart, "Aha. [Aha]. Our desire." Do not let them say, "We have swallowed him up."

Psalm 41:2 LXX(H) Tg (sight confusion PH)
אל דל [וְאֶבְיוֹן] בְּיוֹם

Psalm 41:1 For the Chief Musician. A Psalm by David. Blessed is he who considers the poor [and needy]. The LORD will deliver him in the day of evil.

Psalm 67:4 LXX(H) Ms
כי תִשְׁפֹּט [תבל בצדק תִשְׁפֹּט] עמים במישור

Psalm 67:4 Let the nations be glad and sing for joy, for you will judge [the world in righteousness. You will judge] the peoples with equity, and guide the nations on earth. Selah.

Psalm 73:28 LXX(H) (sight confusion, cf. early square script)
מלאכותיך [בְּשַׁעֲרֵי בת ציון] מַשְׂכִּיל

Psalm 73:28 But it is good for me to come close to God. I have made the LORD my refuge, that I may tell of all your works [in the gates of the daughter of Zion]. 74:1 A contemplation...

Psalm 103:20 Hebrew Mss LXX (sight confusion)
יהוה [כֹּל] מַלְאָכָיו

Psalm 103:20 Praise the LORD, [all] you angels of his, who are mighty in strength, who fulfill his word, obeying the voice of his word.

Psalm 118:6 LXX(H) Syr
יהוה לִי [בְּעֹזְרָי] לא אירא

Psalm 118:6 The LORD is my [helper]; I will not fear. What can man do to me?

Psalm 145:13 Hebrew Ms DSS LXX Syr Vg: > MT

ודורֽ [נֶאֱמָן יהוה בכל דבריו וחסיד בכל מעשיוֽ] סוֹמֵךְ יהוה

Psalm 145:13 Your kingdom is an everlasting kingdom. Your dominion endures throughout all generations. [The LORD is faithful in all his words, and gracious in all his deeds.]

Proverbs 11:16 LXX(H)

אשת חן תתמך כבוד [וכסא קלון שנאת ישר הון
עצלים יחסרו] ועריצים יתמכו עשר:

Proverbs 11:16 A gracious woman obtains honor, [and she who hates virtue makes a throne for dishonor. The slothful become destitute,] and ruthless men grab wealth.

Proverbs 11:31 LXX(H)

הן הצדיק במאמץ נושע רשע וחוטא [אָנָה יראה]: אַהַב

Proverbs 11:31 Behold, if the righteous is saved with difficulty, [where will appear] the ungodly and the sinner?

Isaiah 2:12 LXX(H)

כל נשא [וגבה] וַשָׁפֵל

Isaiah 2:12 For there will be a day of the LORD of hosts for all that is proud and haughty, and for all that is lifted up [and high]; and it shall be brought low:

Isaiah 10:22 LXX(H)

שאר יושע כי [מלה] מלאון וחרוץ שוטף צדקה

Isaiah 10:22 For though your people, Israel, are as the sand of the sea, a remnant will be saved. For he will fulfill [the word] and decisively, overflowing in righteousness.

Isaiah 11:10 LXX(H)

עמד לנשיא [עַל] עַמִים אליו

Isaiah 11:10 And in that day there will be a root of Jesse, one who stands up to rule [over] the peoples; to him will the nations seek, and his resting place will be glorious.

Isaiah 28:16 LXX(H) (sight confusion)
והמאמין [עליו] לא יבוש

Isaiah 28:16 Therefore thus says the LORD, "Look, I am laying in Zion a stone for a foundation, a tried stone, a precious cornerstone of a sure foundation, and whoever believes [in him] will not be put to shame.

Isaiah 29:13 LXX(H)
רחק ממני ותהו יראתם אתי [מלמדים] מצות אנשים ומלמדיה:

Isaiah 29:13 And the Lord said, "Because these people draw near with their mouth and honor me with their lips, but they have removed their heart far from me, and in vain do they worship me, [teaching] the commandments and instructions of men.

Isaiah 40:5 LXX(H) OL Mss (sight confusion)
יחדו [בישע אלהים] כי פי יהוה דבר

Isaiah 40:5 And the glory of the LORD will be revealed, and all flesh will see [the salvation of God] together; for the mouth of the LORD has spoken it."

Isaiah 40:7-8 MT DSS(corr.) LXX Mss: > Hebrew
Mss LXX DSS* (Not counted in totals)
השדה: יבש חציר נבל ציץ [כי רוח יהוה נשבה בו אכן חציר
העם: יבש חציר נבל ציץ] ודבר יהוה יקום לעולם:

Isaiah 40:7 The grass withers, the flower fades, [because the breath of the LORD blows on it. Surely the people are like grass. **8** The grass withers, the flower fades;] but the word of the LORD stands forever."

Isaiah 47:4 LXX(H) OL
אדם: [אמר] גאלנו

Isaiah 47:4 [says] our Redeemer; the LORD of hosts is his name, the Holy One of Israel.

Isaiah 66:21 DSS LXX
אקח [לי] לכהנים

Isaiah 66:21 And I will also take some of them [for myself] as priests and Levites," says the LORD.

Jeremiah 4:29 LXX(H)
כל העיר באו [במערות ויחבאו] בעבים

Jeremiah 4:29 Every city flees for the noise of the horsemen and archers; they go [into caves, and they hide themselves] in the thickets, and climb up on the rocks; every city is forsaken, and not a man dwells therein.

Jeremiah 5:19 Syr(H)
אליהם [כה אמר יהוה] כאשר

Jeremiah 5:19 It will happen, when you say, 'Why has the LORD our God done all these things to us?' Then you shall say to them, '[Thus says the LORD,] Just like you have forsaken me, and served foreign gods in your land, so you shall serve strangers in a land that is not yours.'

Jeremiah 44:19 LXX(H) Mss Syr
תמנו: [והנשם אמרו כי] וכי אנחנו

Jeremiah 44:19 [And the women said,] "When we burned incense to the queen of heaven, and poured out drink offerings to her, did we make her cakes to worship her, and pour out drink offerings to her, without our husbands?"

Joel 2:19 DSS
והיצהר [ואכלתם] ושבעתם אתו

Joel 2:19 The LORD answered his people, "Behold, I will send you grain, new wine, and oil, [and you will eat] and you will be satisfied with them; and I will no more make you a reproach among the nations.

Ezekiel 40:48 LXX(H)
ורחב השער [ארבע עשרי אמה וכתפות השער] שלש

Ezekiel 40:48 Then he brought me to the porch of the house, and measured each post of the porch, five cubits on this side, and five cubits on that side. And the breadth of the gate [was fourteen cubits, and the sides of the gate] were three cubits on this side, and three cubits on that side.

Daniel 5:3 Vg(H) Theodotion
דהבא [וכספא] די

Daniel 5:3 Then they brought the gold [and silver] vessels that were taken out of the temple of the house of God which was in Jerusalem; and the king and his nobles, his wives and his concubines, drank from them.

Hosea 4:3 LXX(H)
השדה [וברמש האדמה] ובעוף

Hosea 4:3 Therefore the land mourns, and all those who dwell in it will waste away, along with the animals of the field [and the creeping things of the earth] and the birds of the sky, and even the fish of the sea will be taken away.

Amos 1:3 DSS LXX
הברזל את [הרות] הגלעד:

Amos 1:3 Thus says the LORD: "For three transgressions of Damascus, yes, for four, I will not turn away its punishment; because they have threshed [the pregnant women of] Gilead with threshing instruments of iron;

Habakkuk 1:5 LXX(H)
ראו בוגדים והביטו והתמהו תמהו [וָשֹׁמּוּ] כִּי [אָנֹכִי]
פעל פעל בימיכם אשר לא תאמינו כי יספר

Habakkuk 1:5 "Look, you scoffers, and watch, and be utterly amazed, [and perish]; for [I am] working a work in your days which you will not believe though it is told you.

Haggai 1:11 Hebrew Mss LXX Syr Tg Vg
ועל [כל] אשר

Haggai 1:11 I called for a drought on the land, and on the mountains, and on the grain, and on the new wine, on the oil, and on [all] what the ground produces, and on men, and on livestock, and on all the labor of the hands."

Haplography List: New Testament

Matthew 2:18 C D (E) K L M N S W Gamma Delta Pi (Omega) 0233 f13 33 892 1071 Byz (lat(d)) syr(s.c.h) arm aeth geo slav; (Diatess(arm)), Or, Proc: > Aleph B Z 0250 f1 279 372 1491 pc L2211 Lat syr(p) sa bo; Ju, Mac/Sy, Hes.

2:18 φωνη εν Ραμα ηκουσθη [θρην**οσ και**] κλαυθμ**οσ και** οδυρμοσ πολυσ Ραχηλ κλαιουσα τα τεκνα αυτησ και ουκ ηθελεν παρακληθηναι οτι ουκ εισιν 19 τελευτησαντοσ

Matthew 2:18 "A voice was heard in Ramah, [lamentation and] weeping and great mourning, Rachel weeping for her children; and she would not be comforted, because they are no more."

Matthew 5:22 Aleph(2) D K L W Gamma Delta Theta Pi f1 f13 33 892 1241 al Byz Lect lat(a.b.c.d.f.ff1.g1.h.k.l.q) vg(Mss) syr(s.c.p.h.pal) sa bo mae arm aeth(th) geo slav; Ir(lat), Or(Mss), Eus, Bas, Ps-Ju, Chr, Cyp, Cyr, Thret: > p64 Aleph* B 1292 lat(aur) vg aeth(Ms); Or(Mss), Hier(Mss)

5:22 εγω δε λεγω υμιν οτι πασ ο οργιζομενοσ τω αδελφω αυτου [**εικη**] **ε**νοχοσ εσται τη κρισει οσ δ αν ειπη τω αδελφω αυτου ρακα ενοχοσ εσται τω συνεδριω οσ δ αν ειπη μωρε ενοχοσ εσται εισ την γεενναν του πυροσ

Matthew 5:22 But I tell you, that everyone who is angry with his brother [without cause] will be in danger of the judgment; and whoever will say to his brother, 'Raqa,' will be in danger of the council; and whoever will say, 'You fool,' will be in danger of the fire of hell.

Matthew 6:25 B W f13 33 al (Byz) lat(aur.c.f.g1.h.q) sa(Mss) mae1 bo arm(Mss) geo(1.(B)) slav; Or, Bas(1/2), Eva, Nil, Marc. [NA28]: > Aleph f1 22* 372 892 vg Lat(a.b.ff1.k.l) syr(c.pal(mss)) sa(pt) mae-2 arm(Mss); Diatess(syr), Ath, Chr, Cyr

6:25 δια τουτο λεγω υμιν μη μεριμνατε τη ψυχη υμων **τι** φαγ**ητε** [η **τι** πι**ητε**] μηδε τω σωματι υμων τι ενδυσησθε ουχι η ψυχη πλειον εστιν τησ τροφησ και το σωμα του ενδυματοσ

Matthew 6:25 Therefore I tell you, do not be anxious about your life, what you will eat [or what you will drink]; or about your body, what you will wear. Is not life more than food, and the body more than clothing?

Matthew 10:8 Aleph* B C* D N P W Delta Sigma Phi 0281(vid) f1 f13(pt) 33 565 892 al vg Lat vg syr(s.h) bo aeth geo(A) arab : > C(1) E F G K L M S U X Y Gamma Theta Pi Omega f13(pt) 579 700* 1071 al Byz lat(f) syr(p.pal) sa mae1 aeth-2(mss) arm geo(1.B); Eus, Bas

10:8 ασθενουντας θεραπευετε [νεκρουσ εγειρετε] λεπρουσ καθαριζετε δαιμονια εκβαλλετε δωρεαν ελαβετε δωρεαν δοτε

Matthew 10:8 Heal the sick, [raise the dead,] cleanse the lepers, cast out demons. Freely you received, freely give.

Matthew 10:37 Aleph C E F G K L M S U W(supp) Delta Theta Pi Omega 33 565 1582 al f1 f13 Byz: > B D 983 syr(h) mae2 (Not counted in totals)
Matthew 10:38: > M*
Matthew 10:37b + 38: p19

10:37 ο φιλων πατερα η μητερα υπερ εμε **ουκ εστιν μου αξιοσ** [και ο φιλων υιον η θυγατερα υπερ εμε **ουκ εστιν μου αξιοσ**] 38 [και οσ ου λαμβανει τον σταυρον αυτου και ακολουθει οπισω μου **ουκ εστιν μου αξιοσ**] 39 ο ευρων

Matthew 10:37 He who loves father or mother more than me is not worthy of me; [and he who loves son or daughter more than me is not worthy of me] **38** [And whoever does not take his cross and follow after me, is not worthy of me].

Matthew 12:15 C D E G K L S U W X Y Gamma Delta Theta Pi Omega 0281 f1 f13 33 565 892 al Byz Lect lat(d.f.h.(q)) syr(p.h) sa(Ms) bo arm (aeth) geo slav; Or, Chr. [NA28]: > Aleph B 372 873 Lat(a.aur.b.c.ff1.g1.k.l) vg (syr(s.c))

12:15 ο δε Ιησουσ γνουσ ανεχωρησεν εκειθεν και ηκολουθησαν αυτω [οχλοι] πολλοι και εθεραπευσεν αυτουσ παντασ

Matthew 12:15 But Jesus, perceiving that, withdrew from there. [Large] crowds followed him, and he healed them all,

Matthew 12:47 Aleph(1) C D E F G K M S U W Y Z Delta Theta Pi Omega f1 f13 33 892 1582 al Byz Lect Lat(a.aur.b.c.d.f.ff2.g1.h.l.q) vg syr(p.h) mae1 bo arm aeth geo slav; Diatess, Or(lat) Chr(lem). [NA28]: > Aleph B L Gamma 579 597 L387 lat(ff1.k) syr(s.c) sa mae2

12:46–47 ετι αυτου λαλουντοσ τοισ οχλοισ ιδου η μητηρ και οι αδελφοι αυτου εειστηκεισαν εξω ζητουντεσ αυτω **λαλησαι** 47 [ειπεν δε τισ αυτω ιδου η μητηρ σου και οι αδελφοι σου εξω εστηκασιν ζητουντεσ σοι **λαλησαι**] 48 ο δε

Matthew 12:46-47 While he was yet speaking to the crowds, suddenly his mother and his brothers stood outside, seeking to speak to him. 47 [Then one said to him, "Look, your mother and your brothers stand outside, seeking to speak to you."]

Matthew 14:30 B(1) C D E F G K L M P S U (W) Y Gamma Delta Theta Pi Omega 0106 f1 f13 579 700 892 al Byz Lect Latt(a.aur.b.c.d.e.f.ff1.ff2.g1.h.l.q) vg syr(s.c.p.h.pal) (mae) arm aeth geo slav; Or, Bas Chr. [NA28]: > Aleph B* 073 33 vg(Ms) sa bo fay

14:30 βλεπων δε τ<u>ον</u> ανεμ<u>ον</u> [ισχυρ<u>ον</u>] εφοβηθη και αρξαμενοσ καταποντιζεσθαι εκραξεν λεγων κυριε σωσον με

Matthew 14:30 But when he saw the [strong] wind, he was afraid, and beginning to sink, he yelled, saying, "Lord, save me."

Matthew 15:6 C E F G K L M N S U W X Y Gamma Delta Theta Pi 0106 0233 f1 597 1006 1342 Byz Lect Lat(aur.(b).(c).f.ff1.(q)) vg(Mss) syr((s).p.h) (mae) (bo) (arm) aeth (geoA); (Diatess(syr)), (Chr), Cyr(2/5): > Aleph B D Omega lat(a.d.e) syr(c) sa geo(2A); Or(lat)

15:6 ου μη τιμησει **τ<u>ου</u> πατ<u>ερα</u> α<u>υτου</u>** [η **τ<u>ην</u>** μη**τ<u>ερα</u> α<u>υτου</u>**] και ηκυρωσατε τον λογον του θεου δια την παραδοσιν υμων

Matthew 15:6 he is not to honor his father [or his mother].' You have made the word of God void because of your tradition.

Matthew 15:14 Aleph(2a) L Z Theta 0233 f1 f13 33 700 1424 al Lat(a.aur.c.e.f.ff1.
ff2.g1.l) vg syr(p.h) mae bo(Mss) arm aeth(th) geo; Or(gr.lat), Bas, Cyr, Thret).
[NA28]: > (Aleph) B D (K) 0237 lat(d) sa bo(Mss) fay(vid); Epiph

15:14 αφετε αυτουσ τυφλοι εισιν οδηγοι [τυφλων] τυφλοσ δε τυφλον εαν οδηγη
αμφοτεροι εισ βοθυνον πεσουνται

Matthew 15:14 Leave them alone. They are blind guides [of the blind]. If the blind
guide the blind, both will fall into a pit."

Matthew 15:15 C D K L W Gamma Theta 0106 0233 0281 33 1241 1342 Byz Lect Lat(a.
aur.c.d.e.f.ff1.ff2.g1.l.q) vg syr(s.c.p.h) sa(Ms) arm aeth geo slav; Bas, Chr. [NA28]: >
Aleph B Zvid f1 579 700 892 vg(Mss) sa bo; Or, Cyr

15:15 αποκριθεισ δε ο πετροσ ειπεν αυτω φρασον ημιν την παραβολ**ην** [ταυτ**ην**]
16 ο δε ειπεν ακμην και υμεισ ασυνετοι εστε

Matthew 15:15 And answering, Peter said to him, "Explain [this] parable to us."

Matthew 18:15 (aural hpgr) D K L N W X Gamma Delta Theta 078 f13 28 892
1241 al Byz Lect(pt) Lat(a.aur.b.c.d.e.f.ff1.n2.g1.h.l.n.q.(r1)) vg syr(s.c.p.h) mae1,2
bo(pt) arm aeth geo slav(Mss); Bas(Ms), Chr(Mss). [NA28]: > Aleph B 0281 1
579 sa bo(pt) slav(Mss); Cyr

18:15 Εαν δε αμαρτ**ηση** [εισ **σε**] ο αδελφοσ σου υπαγε ελεγξον αυτον μεταξυ σου
και αυτου μονου εαν σου ακουση εκερδησασ τον αδελφον σου

Matthew 18:15 "If your brother sins [against you], go, show him his fault between
you and him alone. If he listens to you, you have gained back your brother.

Matthew 18:29 E F H K M S U W Y Gamma Delta Pi Omega 33 565 1241 f13
Byz lat(f.q) syr(p.h) mae1,2 arm: > Aleph B C* D G L Theta 058 579 700 1424
pc f1 Lat(a.b.c.e.ff2.g1.h) vg syr(s.c) sa bo

18:29 πεσων ουν ο συνδουλο**σ αυτου** [εισ τουσ ποδα**σ αυτου**] παρεκαλει αυτον
λεγων μακροθυμησον επ εμοι και αποδωσω σοι

Matthew 18:29 "So his fellow servant fell down [at his feet] and begged him,
saying, 'Have patience with me, and I will repay you all.'

Matthew 19:9 B Z 28 892 1342 al Byz Lect lat(aur.c.f.q) vg syr(p.h) arm aeth geo; Or(lat1/2), Bas, Cyr (γαμησασ | γαμων p25 C* E F G H K M N O U W Gamma Delta Theta 078 0233 f1 f13 33 pc bo mae1 slav; Spec): > Aleph C(3) K L 1241 1546 lat(a.b.d.e.ff1.ff2.g1.h.l.r1) vg(Ms) syr(s.c) sa bo(Ms); Or

19:9 λεγω δε υμιν οτι οσ αν απολυση την γυναικα αυτου μη επι πορνεια και γαμηση αλλην **μοιχαται** [και ο απολελυμενην γαμησασ **μοιχαται**] 10 λεγουσιν

Matthew 19:9 I tell you that whoever divorces his wife, except for sexual immorality, and marries another, commits adultery. [And he who marries her when she is divorced commits adultery.]"

Matthew 19:11 Aleph C D K L N W Z Gamma Delta Theta 078 0233 f13 33 579 1342 al Byz Lect Lat(a.aur.b.c.d.f.ff1.ff2.g1.h.l.q.(r1)) vg syr(s.c.p.h) sa mae bo arm aeth(pp Ms) geo slav; Cl, Or(lat), Bas, Thret. [NA28]: > B f1 892* L184 lat(e) syr(pal) bo(Mss) aeth(ro); Or, Apo, Theod, JohnD(vid)

19:11 ο δε ειπεν αυτοισ ου παντεσ χωρουσιν τον λογ**ον** [τουτ**ον**] αλλ οισ δεδοται

Matthew 19:11 But he said to them, "Not all men can receive [this] saying, but those to whom it is given.

Matthew 19:29 Aleph C E F G H K L M S U W X Gamma Delta Theta f13 33 892 1424 al Byz Lect Lat(aur.c.f.g1.h.l.q) vg syr((c).p.h) sa bo mae1.2 arm aeth geo slav; Bas, GrNy, Cyr: > B lat(a.n) syr(pal); Chr

19:29 και πασ οστισ αφηκεν οικιασ η αδελφουσ η αδελφασ η πατερα **η** μητερ**α [η** γυναικ**α] η** τεκνα η αγρουσ ενεκεν του εμου ονοματοσ πολλαπλασιονα ονοματοσ μου εκατονταπλασιονα λημψεται και ζωην αιωνιον κληρονομησει

Matthew 19:29 Everyone who has left houses, or brothers, or sisters, or father, or mother, [or wife,] or children, or lands, for my name's sake, will receive one hundred times, and will inherit eternal life.

Matthew 20:16 C D E F G H K N Wsupp Gamma Theta Pi 0300 f1 (f13) 33 579 1241 al Byz Lect Latt(aur.b.(c).d.e.f.ff2.g1.h.(l).n.(q) vg syr(s.c.p.h.pal) mae bo(pt) arm aeth geo slav; Chr: > Aleph B L Z 085 892* 1342 pc sa bo(pt); Diatess

20:16 ουτωσ εσονται οι εσχατοι πρωτοι και οι πρωτοι εσχα<u>τοι</u> [πο<u>λλ</u>οι γαρ εισιν κλητοι ολιγοι δε ε<u>κλεκτοι</u>] 17 με<u>λλ</u>ων δε

Matthew 20:16 So the last will be first, and the first last [for many are called, but few are chosen.]

Matthew 21:44 Aleph B C E F G H K L M S U W X Y Z Delta (Theta) Pi Omega 0102 0233 f1 f13 28 565 892 al Byz Lect lat(aur.c.f.g1.(h).l.q) vg syr(c.p.h) sa bo mae arm aeth geo slav; Diatess(arab), Chr, Cyr. [NA28]: > p104vid D 33 lat(a.b.d.e.ff1.ff2.r1) syr(s); Ir(lat), Or, Eus(syr)

καρπουσ <u>αυτ</u>ησ 44 [<u>και</u> ο πεσων επι τον λιθον τουτον συνθλασθησεται εφ ον δ αν πεση λικμησει <u>αυτ</u>ον] 45 <u>και</u> ακουσαντεσ

Matthew 21:44 [He who falls on this stone will be broken to pieces; but on whomever it will fall, it will crush him.]

Matthew 23:4 B D(2) E F G H K M S U W Y Gamma Delta Theta Pi Omega 0102 0107 Pi f13 28 33 1424 al Byz Lect lat(aur.c.d.f.ff1.g1.l.q) vg syr(h.pal(Mss)) sa (mae1) arm geo slav; Chr. [NA28]: > (Aleph) L f1 205 892 lat(a.b.e.ff2.h) syr(s.c.p) bo mae2; Ir(lat), Or(lat)

23:4 δεσμευουσιν δε φορτια βαρε<u>α</u> [<u>και</u> δυσβαστακτ<u>α</u>] <u>και</u> επιτιθεασιν επι τουσ ωμουσ των ανθρωπων αυτοι δε τω δακτυλω αυτων ου θελουσιν κινησαι αυτα

Matthew 23:4 For they bind heavy [and hard to bear] burdens, and lay them on men's shoulders; but they themselves will not lift a finger to help them.

Matthew 23:13(14) E F G H K M S U W Y Gamma Delta Pi Omega 0102 0107 28 565 1241 al Byz Lect lat(f) vg(cl) syr((c).p.h.(pal(Mss))) bo(pt) aeth slav; Chr: > Aleph B D L Z Theta f1 33 892 1344 Lat(a.aur.d.e.ff1.g1) vg(st.ww) syr(s.pal(Ms)) sa mae bo(pt) arm geo; Or, Eusebian Canons, Cyr

23:13(14) [**Ουαι δε υμιν γραμματεισ και φαρισαιοι υποκριται οτι κ**ατεσθιετε τασ οικιασ των χηρων και προφασει μακρα προσευχομενοι δια τουτο ληψεσθε περισσοτερον κριμα]

23:14(13)**Ουαι δε υμιν γραμματεισ και φαρισαιοι υποκριται οτι κ**λειετε την βασιλειαν των ουρανων εμπροσθεν των ανθρωπων υμεισ γαρ ουκ εισερχεσθε ουδε τουσ εισερχομενουσ αφιετε εισελθειν

Matthew 23:13(14) [Woe to you, scribes and Pharisees, hypocrites. For you devour the houses of widows, and for show make long prayers. Therefore you will receive greater condemnation.]

Matthew 24:7 C F G H K L M Q S W Y Gamma Delta Theta Pi Omega 0102 f1 f13 28 565 1582 Byz Lect lat(h.q) vg syr(p.h) bo mae1 arm geo slav; (Hipp), Or(lat): > (Aleph) B D E* 892 lat(a.b.d.e.ff2.r1) syr(s) sa mae-2; Or(vid)

24:7 εγερθησεται γαρ εθνοσ επι εθνοσ και βασιλεια επι βασιλειαν και εσονται λ**ιμοι [και** λο**ιμοι] και** σεισμοι κατα τοπουσ

Matthew 24:7 For nation will rise against nation, and kingdom against kingdom; and there will be famines [and plagues] and earthquakes in various places.

Matthew 24:39 Aleph E G H K L M S U W Delta Theta Pi Omega 067 f1 f13 33 565 1582 Byz Lat(aur.c.e.f.ff2.g1.l) vg syr(h). [NA28]: > B D F 892 lat(a.b.d.ff1.h.q.r1) vg(Mss) syr(s.p) sa bo

24:39 και ουκ εγνωσαν εωσ ηλθεν ο κατακλυσμοσ και ηρεν απαντασ ουτωσ εστ**αι** [κ**αι**] η παρουσια του υιου του ανθρωπου

Matthew 24:39 and they did not know until the flood came, and took them all away, [so] will be the coming of the Son of Man.

Matthew 26:3 E F G K M U Gamma Pi 0255 22 28 579 pc Byz lat(e.f.ff2.h.q.rl) syr(p.h) arm; Or, Chr: > p45 Aleph A B D L Theta 0293 f1 f13 33vid 892 1424 pc Lat(a.aur.b.d.ff1.g1.l) vg syr(s) sa bo mae2

26:3 τοτε συνηχθησαν οι αρχιερ**εισ** [**και οι** γραμματ**εισ**] **και οι** πρεσβυτεροι του λαου εισ την αυλην του αρχιερεωσ του λεγομενου καιαφα

Matthew 26:3 Then the chief priests [and the scribes] and the elders of the people gathered together in the court of the high priest, who was called Caiaphas.

Matthew 27:24 Aleph E F G K H L M S U W Gamma Pi Omega f1 f13 33 579 892 al Byz Lect lat(aur.c.f.ff1.g1.h.l.q) vg syr(p.h) sa(pt) bo mae1.2 arm aeth geo1 slav; Apos. Const., CyrJ, Cyr: > B D Theta L844 lat(a.b.d.ff2.rl) vg(Ms) syr(s) (sa(pt)) geo2; Or(lat), Ps-Athan, Chr

27:24 ιδων δε ο Πιλατοσ οτι ουδεν ωφελει αλλα μαλλον θορυβοσ γινεται λαβων υδωρ απενιψατο τασ χειρασ απεναντι του οχλου λεγων αθωοσ ειμι απο <u>του</u> αιματοσ [**του** δικαι**ου**] **του**του υμεισ οψεσθε

Matthew 27:24 So Pilate, seeing that nothing was being gained, but rather that a disturbance was starting, took water and he washed his hands before the crowd, saying, "I am innocent of the blood of this [righteous] man. Look to it yourselves."

Mark 1:1 Aleph(1) (A) B D (E F G H K) L (M U) W (Y) Gamma Delta Pi Omega f1 f13 33 892 1424 al Byz Lect Latt vg syr(p.h) sa bo aeth geo2 goth slav; Ir(lat2/3), Ambr, Hier. [NA28]: > Aleph* Theta 28(c) pc L2211 syr(pal) sa(Ms) arm geo1; Or(gr.lat), Ast, Ser, CyrJ, Sev, Hes

1:1 Αρχη τ<u>ου</u> ευαγγελι<u>ου</u> Ιησ<u>ου</u> Χριστ<u>ου</u> [υι<u>ου</u> θε<u>ου</u>] 2 καθωσ

or ΙΥΧ**Υ**[ΥΥΘ**Υ**]Κ

Mark 1:1 The beginning of the Good News of Jesus (the) Messiah, [the Son of God].

Mark 1:40 Aleph(2) L Theta f1 579 892 1241 al two lect lat(e.f.l.q) vg syr(s.p) arm aeth geo1 slav; Aug [NA28] (+ αυτον A C E F K M S U Delta Pi Omega 0130 0233 f13 33vid 1424 Byz Lect lat((q)) syr(h.pal) geo2; Bas): > B D G W 124 pc five Lect lat(a.aur.b.c.d.ff2.r1) vg(Ms) (sa(Mss))

1:40 και ερχεται προσ αυτον λεπροσ παρακαλων αυτο<u>ν [και</u> γονυπετω<u>ν] και</u> λεγων αυτω οτι εαν θελησ δυνασαι με καθαρισαι

Mark 1:40 And a leper came to him, begging him, [and knelt down] and said to him, "If you want to, you can make me clean."

Mark 2:16 p88 A C E F H K M S U Gamma Omega f1 33 892 1505 al Byz Lect lat(c.l.q) vg(Ms) syr(p.h) sa(Ms) goth; (Diatess): > (Aleph) B D W Pi 213 1704* 2159 al lat(a.b.d.e.ff2.r1)

2:16 και οι γραμματεισ των φαρισαιων ιδοντεσ οτι εσθιει μετα των αμαρτωλων και τελωνων ελεγον τοισ μαθηταισ αυτου οτι μετα των τελωνων και αμαρτωλων εσθι<u>ει [και</u> πιν<u>ει]</u> 17 <u>και</u> ακουσασ

Mark 2:16 And the scribes of the Pharisees, when they saw him eating with the tax collectors and sinners, said to his disciples, "Why is it that he eats [and drinks] with tax collectors and sinners?"

Mark 3:15 A C(2) D F G H K M P S U W Y Gamma Pi Omega f1 f13 33 579 1241 al Byz Latt(aur.b.d.f.ff2.i.l.q.r1.t) vg syr(s.p.h) arm goth: > Aleph B C* L Delta 565 892 pc sa bo geo

3:15 και εχειν εξουσιαν [θεραπευ<u>ειν τασ</u> νοσουσ και] εκβαλλ<u>ειν τα</u> δαιμονια

Mark 3:15 and to have authority to [heal sicknesses and to] cast out demons.

Mark 3:16 Aleph B C* Delta 565 579 (1342) sa(Ms). [NA28]: > A C(2) D E F G H K L M P S U (W) Y Theta Pi Omega f1 28 33 1424 al Byz Latt(aur.b.d.f.ff2.i.l.q.r1.t) vg syr(s.p.h) bo arm geo goth slav; Aug

3:16 [<u>και επ</u>οιησ<u>εν</u> τουσ δωδεκα] <u>και επ</u>εθηκ<u>εν</u> ονομα τω Σιμωνι Πετρον

Mark 3:16 [And he appointed the Twelve.] And to Simon he gave the name Peter;

Mark 6:51 A E F G K M N S U W X Gamma Pi Omega f13 33 579 1241 al Byz Lect Latt(a.(aur).(c).d.f.ff2.i.l.q.rl) vg syr(h); slav. [NA28]: > Aleph B L Delta 892 (syr(s.p)) sa bo geo1

6:51 και ανεβη προσ αυτουσ εισ το πλοιον και εκοπασεν ο ανεμοσ και λιαν [εκ περισσου] εν εαυτοισ εξισταντο

Mark 6:51 And he got into the boat with them, and the wind ceased. And they were completely [profusely] astonished among themselves;

Mark 7:4 A D E F G H K M S U W X Y Gamma Theta Pi f1 f13 33 579 892 al Byz Lect Lat vg syr(p.h) sa(Mss) arm aeth geo goth slav; Or. [NA28]: > p45vid Aleph B L Delta 28* 1342 L292 (syr(s)) sa(Ms) bo

7:4 και απ αγορασ εαν μη βαπτισωνται ουκ εσθιουσιν και αλλα πολλα εστιν α παρελαβον κρατειν βαπτισμουσ ποτηριων και ξεστων και χαλκι**ων** [**και** κλιν**ων**] 5 **και** επερωτωσιν

Mark 7:4 They do not eat when they come from the marketplace unless they wash. And there are many other things which they have received and hold to, the washing of cups and pitchers and copper vessels [and dining couches].

Mark 9:29 p45(vid) A C D E F G H K L M N S U V W X Y Gamma Theta Pi Sigma Phi Psi Omega 0211 f1 f13 33 892 1342 al Byz Lect Lat(a.aur.b.c.d.f.ff2.i.l.q.rl) vg syr(s.p.h.pal) sa bo aeth arm geo2 goth slav; Diatess(arab), Tert, Cl(hom), Juv, Ast, Hil, Ath, Bas, Ambr, Chr, Hier, Aug: > Aleph* B Delta* 0274 lat(k) geo1

9:29 και ειπεν αυτοισ τουτο το γενοσ εν ουδενι δυναται εξελθειν ει μη εν προσευχη [**και** νηστεια] 30 **κα**κειθεν εξελθοντεσ

Mark 9:29 And he said to them, "This kind can come out by nothing, except by prayer [and fasting]."

Mark 9:49 A (C) E F G H K N S U Y X Gamma (Theta) (Psi) Omega f13 892 1241 1424 al Byz Lect Lat(f.l.q) (vg) syr(p.h) bo(pt) aeth goth slav: > Aleph B L M (W) Delta Pi 0274 f1 28* 579 700 al syr(s) sa bo(pt) arm geo; (TheoHer), Did

9:49 πασ γαρ πυρι **αλισθησεται** [και πασα θυσια αλ**ι αλισθησεται**] 50 **κα**λον

Mark 9:49 For everyone will be salted with fire, [and every sacrifice will be salted with salt].

Mark 10:7 (A) (C) D E F G H K (L) M (N) S U W X Y Gamma Theta Pi Omega al (f1) f13 28 1241 1424 al Byz Lat(b.d.ff2.l.(q)) vg syr(p.h) sa bo fay arm aeth geo slav. [NA28]: > Aleph B Psi 892* syr(s) goth

10:7 ενεκεν τουτου καταλειψει ανθρωποσ τον πατερα αυτου και την μητερα [**και** προσκολληθησεται προσ την γυναικα αυτου] 8 **και** εσονται

Mark 10:7 For this cause a man will leave his father and mother, [and will join to his wife,]

Mark 10:24 A C (D) E F G H K M N S U X Y Gamma (Theta) Pi Omega 0233 (f1) (f13) 579 892 1342 Byz Lect Lat(aur.f.l.q) vg syr(s.p.h) bo(pt) arm aeth geo goth slav; (Diatess), Cl: > Aleph B W Delta Psi* lat(k) sa bo(pt)

10:24 οι δε μαθηται εθαμβουντο επι τοισ λογοισ αυτου ο δε Ιησουσ παλιν αποκριθεισ λεγει αυτοισ τεκνα πωσ δυσκολον εστ**ιν** [τους πεποιθοτασ επι χρημασ**ιν**] εις την βασιλειαν του θεου εισελθειν

Mark 10:24 The disciples were amazed at his words. But Jesus answered again and said to them, "Children, how hard it is [for those who trust in riches] to enter the kingdom of God.

Mark 11:26 A C D E Fvid G H K M N X Y Gamma Theta Pi Omega 0233 f1 f13 33 579 1241 al Byz Lect Lat(a.aur.b.c.d.f.ff2.i.q.r1) vg syr(p.h) bo(pt) aeth goth slav; Cyp, Spec > Aleph B L W Delta Psi 565 700 892 pc lat(k.l) syr(s.pal) sa bo(pt) arm geo

11:25 και οταν στηκετε προσευχομενοι αφιετε ει τι εχετε κατα τινοσ ινα και **ο πατηρ υμων ο εν τοισ ουρανοισ αφη** υμιν **τα παραπτωματα υμων** 26 [ει δε υμεισ ουκ αφιετε ουδε **ο πατηρ υμων ο εν τοισ ουρανοισ αφησει τα παραπωματα υμων**] 27 και ερχονται

Mark 11:26 [But if you do not forgive, neither will your Father in heaven forgive your transgressions.]

Mark 12:33 A E F G H K S M U X Gamma Pi Omega 087 f13 22 700 1424 Byz Lat(b.c.ff2.i.l.q) vg syr(p.h) sa(Ms) (bo(Ms)) aeth goth; Hil: > Aleph B L W Delta Theta Psi (f1 579 2542) 892 pc lat(a) sa(Mss) (bo) arm

12:33 και το αγαπαν αυτον εξ ολησ τησ καρδιασ και εξ ολησ τησ συνεσεω**σ και εξ ολησ τησ** [ψυχη**σ και εξ ολησ τησ**] ισχυοσ και το αγαπαν τον πλησιον ωσ εαυτον περισσοτερον εστιν παντων των ολοκαυτωματων και θυσιων

Mark 12:33 and to love him with all the heart, and with all the understanding, and with all the [soul and with all the] strength, and to love his neighbor as himself, is more important than all whole burnt offerings and sacrifices."

Mark 14:19 D E F H K M S U X Y Gamma Theta Pi Omega f1 565 1241 1582 al Byz lat(a.d.f.ff2.i.k.q) syr(h(mg)) arm geo; Or: > Aleph B C L P W Delta Psi lat(aur.l) vg syr(s.p.h) sa bo

14:19 ηρξαντο λυπεισθαι και λεγειν αυτω εισ κατα ει**σ μητι εγω** [και αλλο**σ μητι εγω**] 20 ο δε ειπεν

Mark 14:19 And they began to be sorrowful, and to say to him one by one, "Surely not I?" [And another said, "Surely not I?"]

Mark 15:28 E F H K L M P S U Gamma Delta Theta Pi Omega 083 0250 f1 f13 33 892 1342 al Byz six lect Lat(aur.c.ff2.l.n.r1) vg syr(p.h.pal) (bo(pt)) arm aeth geo goth slav; (Diatess(arm)), Ps-Hipp, Or(vid), Eus, Vig: > Aleph A B C D X Y* Psi 047 pm Lect lat(d.k) syr(s) sa bo(pt)

15:27 ...αυτου 28 [και επληρωθη η γραφη η λεγουσα και μετα ανομων ελογισθη] 29 και οι

Mark 15:28 [And the Scripture was fulfilled which says, "And he was numbered with transgressors."]

Mark 15:39 A C D E G H M N S U W X Gamma Delta Pi Omega 0233 f1 f13 33 579 1342 al Byz Lect Latt(aur.c.ff2.(i).l.n.q) vg syr((s).p.h) aeth (arm) (geo) goth slav; (Or(lat)), Aug: > Aleph B L Psi 083vid 297 892 2430 sa bo

15:39 ιδων δε ο κεντυριων ο παρεστηκως εξ εναντιας αυτου οτι ουτως [κραζας] εξεπνευσεν ειπεν αληθως ουτος ο ανθρωπος υιος θεου ην

Mark 15:39 When the centurion, who stood by opposite him, saw that he [cried out] and breathed his last like this, he said, "Truly this man was the Son of God."

Luke 4:5 A E G H K M S U Y Gamma Delta Theta Lambda Pi Psi Omega 0102 (f13) 33 579 1342 al Byz lat(d.f.ff2.l.q) (vg) vg(cl) syr(p.h) bo(Mss) goth: > Aleph* B L 1241 pc sa(Mss) bo(pt)

4:5 και αναγαγων αυτ**ον** [ο διαβολος εις οπος υψηλ**ον**] εδειξεν αυτω πασας τας βασιλειας της οικουμενης εν στιγμη χρονου

Luke 4:5 And taking him up [to a high mountain the devil] showed him all the kingdoms of the world in a moment of time.

Luke 4:18 A E (F) G H K M S U Y Gamma (Delta Theta) Lambda Pi Psi Omega 0102 0233 f1 33 565 1342 al Byz lat(f) vg(Mss) syr(p.h.pal) bo(Mss) geo slav; Ir(lat), (Hipp), (Cyr), Thret: > Aleph B D L W Xi f13 700 892 al Lat(a. aur.b.c.d.ff2.l.q.rl) vg(ww.st) syr(s) sa bo aeth arm goth; Or(gr.lat), PetA, Eus, Did

4:18 πνευμα κυριου επ εμε ου εινεκεν εχρισεν με ευαγγελισασθαι πτωχοισ απεσταλκεν με [ιασασθ**αι** τουσ συντετριμμενουσ την καρδιαν] κηρυξ**αι** αιχμαλωτοισ αφεσιν και τυφλοισ αναβλεψιν αποστειλαι τεθραυσμενουσ εν αφεσει

Luke 4:18 "The Spirit of the Lord is upon me, because he has anointed me to preach good news to the poor. He has sent me to [heal the brokenhearted, to] proclaim liberty to the captives, recovering of sight to the blind, to deliver those who are crushed,

Luke 6:1 A C D E H K M R S U X Y Gamma Delta Theta Lambda Pi Psi 0233 (f13) 565 892 1342 al Byz Lat(a.aur.d.f.ff2) vg syr(h) arm goth slav; Epiph, Chr, Is: > p4 p75vid Aleph B L W f1 33 579 1241 al lat(b.c.e.l.q.rl) syr(p.h(mg).pal) sa bo(pt) aeth

6:1 Εγενετο δε εν σαββα**τω [δ**ευτεροπρω**τω] δ**ιαπορευεσθαι αυτον δια σποριμων και ετιλλον οι μαθηται αυτου και ησθιον τουσ σταχυασ ψωχοντεσ ταισ χερσιν

Luke 6:1 Now it happened on the [second chief] Sabbath that he was going through the grain fields, and his disciples plucked the heads of grain, and ate, rubbing them in their hands.

Luke 9:59 (overbar hpgr) p45 p75 Aleph A B(2) C E G H K L M N S U W Gamma Delta Theta Lambda Xi Pi Psi 0181 f1 f13 28 33 892 1342 al Byz Lect Lat(a. aur.b.c.e.f.l.q.rl) vg syr(c.p.h.pal) sa bo arm aeth geo slav; Bas. [NA28]: > B* D 180 lat(d) syr(s); Or

9:59 ειπεν δε προσ ετερον ακολουθει μοι ο δε ει $\overline{pe}$ [$\overline{ke}$] επιτρεψον μοι απελθοντι πρωτον θαψαι τον πατερα μου

Luke 9:59 And he said to another, "Follow me." But he said, "[Lord,] allow me first to go and bury my father."

Luke 11:14 A(c) C F G H K M R S W X Y Gamma Delta Theta Psi f13 28 579 1342 al Byz Lect Lat(a2.aur.b.c.f.ff2.i.l.q.r1) vg syr(p.h) aeth geo slav; Cyr(lem). [NA28]: > p45 p75 Aleph A* B L 0211 f1 33 892 1241 al syr(s.c) sa bo arm

11:14 και ην εκβαλλων δαιμονιο<u>ν [κ</u>αι αυτο η<u>ν] κ</u>ωφον εγενετο δε του δαιμονιου εξελθοντοσ ελαλησεν ο κωφοσ και εθαυμασαν οι οχλοι

Luke 11:14 And he was casting out a demon, [and it was] mute. It happened, when the demon had gone out, the mute man spoke; and the crowds marveled.

Luke 12:39 Aleph(1) A B E G H K L M N P Q W Gamma Delta Theta Lambda Pi Psi Omega al 070 f1 f13 579 1241 1342 al Byz Lect Lat(aur.f.l.q) vg syr(p.h.pal) sa(Ms) bo(Mss) aeth geo slav; Bas, Nic: > p75 Aleph* lat(e.i) syr(s.c) sa(Mss) ach arm; Mcion(T)

12:39 τουτο δε γινωσκετε οτι ει ηδει ο οικοδεσποτησ ποια ωρα ο κλεπτησ ερχετ<u>αι</u> [εγρηγορησεν αν κ<u>αι]</u> ουκ αν αφηκεν διορυχθηναι τον οικον αυτου

Luke 12:39 But know this, that if the master of the house had known in what hour the thief was coming, he would [have watched and] not have allowed his house to be broken into.

Luke 16:21 Aleph(2) A (D) E F G H K M P U W X Y Gamma Delta Theta Lambda Pi Psi Omega 0211 (f1) f13 33 579 1241 al Byz Lect lat(a.aur.d.f) vg syr(p.h) sa(Ms) bo(pt) aeth arm geo goth slav; Or(gr,lat), Ad(lat): > p75 Aleph* B L 79* lat(b.c.e.ff2.i.l.q.r1) syr(s.c.pal) sa(Mss) bo(pt); Mcion(A), Cl

16:21 και επιθυμων χορτασθηναι απο <u>των</u> [ψιχιων <u>των]</u> πιπτοντων απο τησ τραπεζησ του πλουσιου αλλα και οι κυνεσ ερχομενοι επελειχον τα ελκη αυτου

Luke 16:21 and desiring to be fed with [the crumbs] that fell from the rich man's table. Yes, even the dogs came and licked his sores.

Luke 17:24 Aleph A K L N W X Gamma Delta Theta Pi Psi f1 f13 28 565 700 892 1010 1241 Byz Lect lat(aur.q.r1) vg syr((s).(c).p.h) bo arm geo slav. [NA28]: > p75 B (D) lat(a) (lat(b.d.e.i)) sa

17:24 ωσπερ γαρ η αστραπη αστραπτουσα εκ τησ υπο τον ουρανον εισ την υπ ουρανον λαμπει ουτωσ εσται ο υιοσ του ανθρωπ<u>ου</u> [εν τη ημερα αυτ<u>ου</u>] 25 πρωτον

Luke 17:24 for as the lightning, when it flashes out of the one part under the sky, shines to the other part under the sky; so will the Son of Man be [in his day].

Luke 19:45 A E G H K M R S U W Pi Omega 33 565 1424 al Byz Lat(aur.f) vg syr(s.c.p) goth: > Aleph B L f1 1 579 1241 pc syr(pal) sa bo geo

19:45 και εισελθων εισ το ιερον ηρξατο εκβαλλειν τουσ πωλου<u>ντασ</u> [εν αυτω και αγοραζο<u>ντασ</u>] 46 λεγων αυτοισ

Luke 19:45 And he entered into the temple, and began to drive out those who were selling [and buying in it],

Luke 22:16 E F G K M P S U (W) X Gamma Delta Lambda Pi Omega 0279 f1 f13 565 892 1582 al Byz Lect Lat(aur.b.c.(d).e.f.ff2.i.(l).q.(r1)) vg arm aeth (geo) slav; Or(lat): > p75vid Aleph B L H Theta 579 1241 seven lect lat(a) sa bo; Apo, Cyr, Tit, Epiph

22:16 λεγω γαρ υμιν ο<u>τι [ου</u>κε<u>τι] ου</u> μη φαγω αυτο εωσ οτου πληρωθη εν τη βασιλεια του θεου

Luke 22:16 for I say to you, I will not eat of it [again] until it is fulfilled in the Kingdom of God."

Luke 22:68 A (D) E G H K M N S U (W) X Y Gamma Delta Lambda Pi Psi Omega 0211 0233 f13 28 700 1071 al Byz Lect Latt((a).aur.b.c.d.(e).ff2.(i).(l).q.r1) vg syr(s.c.p) aeth arm geo slav; Aug: > p75 Aleph B L T 1241 1278* syr(h) bo; Cyr, Ambr

22:68 εαν δε ερωτησω ου μ<u>η απο</u>κριθ<u>ητε</u> [μοι <u>η απο</u>λυσ<u>ητε</u>] 69 απο

Luke 22:68 and if I ask, you will not answer [me, or let me go].

Luke 23:17 Aleph E F G H M (N) S U W X Y Gamma Delta (Theta) Lambda (Psi) Omega f1 f13 28 157 1071 al Byz Lect Lat(aur.b.c.e.f.ff2.l.q.r1) vg syr((s.c.p) h) bo(pt) (sa(Mss) aeth) arm geo slav; Eusebian Canons: > p75 A B K L T Pi 070 0124 0211 892* 1241 lat(a) vg(Ms) sa bo(pt); Diatess(arab)

23:16b–18 ουν αυτον απολυσω 17 [**α**ν**α**γκη**ν δε** ειχεν απολυειν αυτοισ κατα εορτην ενα] 18 **αν**εκραγο**ν δε** παμπληθει λεγοντεσ αιρε τουτον απολυσον δε ημιν τον βαραββαν

Luke 23:17 [Now he had to release one prisoner to them at the feast.]

Luke 23:23 A D E F G H K M N P S U W X Gamma Delta Theta Psi Lambda Omega 0250 f1 f13 157 579 892 al Byz Lect (lat(c.d.f)) syr((s).(c).p.h) bo(Ms) arm aeth geo slav: > p75 Aleph B L 070 130 755 1241 lat(a.aur.b.e.ff2) vg sa bo; Aug

23:23–24 οι δε επεκειντο φωναισ μεγαλαισ αιτουμενοι αυτον σταυρωθηναι και κατισχυον αι φωναι αυτ**ων [και** των απχιερε**ων]** 24 **και** πιλατοσ επεκρινεν γενεσθαι το αιτημα αυτων

Luke 23:23 But they were urgent with loud voices, asking that he might be crucified. And their voices, [and those of the chief priests,] prevailed.

Luke 24:51 p75 Aleph(2) A B C K L W X Delta Theta Pi Psi f1 f13 33 892 1241 al Byz Lect lat(aur.c.f.q.r1) vg syr(p.h.pal) sa bo arm aeth geo2 slav; Sev, (Hes), Aug(2/3): > Aleph* D lat(a.b.d.e.ff2.l) syr(s) geo1; Aug(1/3)

24:51 και εγενετο εν τω ευλογειν αυτον αυτουσ διεστη απ αυτω**ν [και α**νεφερετο εισ τον ουρανο**ν]** 52 **και α**υτοι

Luke 24:51 And it happened, while he blessed them, that he departed from them [and was carried up into heaven].

Luke 24:53 A C(2) F H K M S U W Gamma* Delta Theta Lambda Pi Psi Omega f1 f13 28 33 892 al Byz Lect lat(aur.c.f.q) vg syr(p.h) aeth arm slav; Diatess, (Hes): > p75 Aleph B C* L syr(s.pal) sa bo geo

24:53 και ησαν δια παντοσ εν τω ιερω [αιν**ουντεσ** και] ευλογ**ουντεσ** τον θεον

Luke 24:53 and were continually in the temple, [praising and] blessing God.

Luke 24:53 (A C(2) F H K M S U W Gamma* Delta Theta Lambda Pi Psi Omega f1 f13 28 33 892 al Byz Lect lat(aur.c.f.q) vg syr(p.h) aeth arm slav; Diatess, (Hes): > D lat(a.b.d.e.ff2.l.rl); Aug (not counted in totals)

24:53 και ησαν δια παντοσ εν τω ιερω αιν**ουντεσ** [και ευλογ**ουντεσ**] τον θεον

Luke 24:53 and were continually in the temple, praising [and blessing] God.

John 5:44 Aleph A D K L Delta Theta Pi Psi f1 f13 33 579 1241 al Byz Lect Lat(aur.c.d.e.f.ff2.j.l.q.rl) vg syr(c.p.h.pal) bo(pt) eth geo slav(Ms); Or, Bas, GrNy, Eva: > p66 p75 B W lat(a.b) sa pbo bo(pt) ach2 arm; Cyr(1/5)

5:44 πωσ δυνασθε υμεισ πιστευσαι δοξαν παρα αλληλων λαμβανοντεσ και την δοξαν την παρα τ**ου** μον**ου** [θε**ου**] **ου** ζητειτε

John 5:44 How can you believe, who receive glory from one another, and you do not seek the glory that comes from the only [God]?

John 6:11 Aleph(2) D E F G H K M S U Gamma Delta Theta Lambda Psi Omega f13 28 397 1071 al Byz lat(b.d.e.g1.j) syr(s) ac2 bo(Mss); Cyr: > p28(vid) p66 p75 Aleph* A B L N W Pi 063 0141 f1 33 565 1241 al lat(a.c.f.ff2.q) vg syr(c.p.h) sa pbo bo arm goth

6:11 ελαβεν ουν τουσ αρτουσ ο Ιησουσ και ευχαριστησασ διεδωκεν **τοισ** [μαθηταισ οι δε μαθηται **τοισ**] ανακειμενοισ ομοιωσ και εκ των οψαριων οσον ηθελον 12 ωσ δε ενεπλησθησαν

John 6:11 Jesus took the loaves; and having given thanks, he distributed to [the disciples, and the disciples to] those who were sitting down; likewise also of the fish as much as they desired.

John 7:46 (p66*) (Aleph*) X Delta Theta Psi 0105vid 0141 f1 f13 565 893 1424 al Byz Lect lat(e.f.(ff2).q.rl) vg syr((c).(s).(p).h.(pal)) sa pbo ac2 arm aeth geo goth slav; Ast, Chr: > p66(c) p75 Aleph(2) B L T W 849 vg(Ms) bo; Or.

7:46 απεκριθησαν οι υπηρεται ουδεποτε ελαλησεν ουτωσ **ανθρωποσ** [ωσ ουτοσ ο **ανθρωποσ**] 47 απεκριθησαν

John 7:46 The officers answered, "No man ever spoke like [this man]."

John 10:13 A(c) E F G K M S U Y X Gamma Delta Lambda Pi Psi 0141 0250vid f13 565 700 1424 al Byz Lat(a.b.c.f.ff2.g1.q) vg syr(p.h) goth: > p44vid p45 p66 p75 Aleph A*vid B D L (W) Theta 0211 1 33 (579) 1241 al L253 lat(d.e) syr(s.pal) sa bo aeth arm

10:12b-13 σκορπιζει 13 [ο δε μισθωτοσ φευγει] οτι μισθωτοσ εστιν και ου μελει αυτω περι των προβατων

John 10:13 [And the hired hand flees] because he is a hired hand and the sheep means nothing to him.

John 10:39 p66 Aleph A L W Delta Psi 0141 f1 f13 33 579 1241 al Byz(pt) Lat(a. aur.b.c.e.ff2.l.r1) vg syr(h) sa(Mss); Aug. [NA28]: > p75vid B Theta 28 700 1342 al Byz(pt) vg(Ms) pbo bo (arm) (geo); Or(lem)

10:39 εζητ<u>ουν</u> [ουν] αυτον παλιν πιασαι και εξηλθεν εκ τησ χειροσ αυτων

John 10:39 [Now] they sought again to seize him, and he went out of their hand.

John 12:19 D L Q X Theta Psi 0141 0211 f13 33 892 1424 al Latt(a.b.c.e.f.ff2. g1.q) vg syr(s.p.h**.pal) ac bo arm: > p66* Aleph A B E G H K M S U W Y Delta Lambda Pi Omega 28 565 1582 al Byz sa ac2 goth.

12:19 οι ουν φαρισαιοι ειπαν προσ εαυτουσ θεωρειτε οτι ουκ ωφελειτε ουδεν ιδε ο κοσμ<u>οσ [ολοσ] ο</u>πισω αυτου απηλθεν

John 12:19 The Pharisees therefore said among themselves, "See how you accomplish nothing. Look, the [whole] world has gone after him."

John 13:32 Aleph(2) A C(2) E F G H K M S U Y Delta Theta Lambda Psi Omega f13 28 33 565 al Byz lat(aur(c).e.f.ff2(c).q.r1) vg syr(p) sa pbo bo(pt) arm aeth geo1 goth slav; Or. [NA28]: > p66 Aleph* B C* D L W X Pi f1 lat(a. aur*.b.c.d.ff2*.l.11A.29.47) vg(Mss) syr(s.h.pal) bo(pt) ac2 mf; Cyr, Thret

13:31 οτε ουν εξηλθεν λεγει ιησουσ νυν εδοξασθη ο υιοσ του ανθρωπου και <u>ο θεοσ εδοξασθη εν αυτω</u> 32 [ει <u>ο θεοσ εδοξασθη εν αυτω</u>] και ο θεοσ δοξασει αυτον εν αυτω και ευθυσ δοξασει αυτον

John 13:32 [If God has been glorified in him,] God will also glorify him in himself, and he will glorify him at once.

Acts 4:17 E Hsupp P Psi 056 33 1241 1243 al Byz syr(h); Chr: > p74vid Aleph A B D 1175 1739 Latt vg sa bo aeth arm; Bas.

4:17 αλλ ινα μη επι πλειον διανεμηθη εισ τον λαον [*απειλη*] *απειλη*σωμεθα αυτοισ μηκετι λαλειν επι τω ονοματι τουτω μηδενι ανθρωπων

Acts 4:17 But so this does not spread any further among the people, let us [severely] threaten them, that from now on they do not speak to anyone in this name.

Acts 10:36 p74 Aleph* C D E P Psi 945 1241 2495 pc Byz Lect lat(e) syr(p.h) geo slav; CyrJ, Chr. [NA28]: > Aleph(1) A B 81 614 1739 L1178 Lat(ar.c.d.dem. gig.l.p.ph.ro.t.w) vg sa bo mae arm eth; Hipp, Ath, CyrA

10:36 τον λογ<u>ον</u> [<u>ον</u>] απεστειλεν τοισ υιοισ Ισραηλ ευαγγελιζομενοσ ειρηνην δια Ιησου Χριστου ουτοσ εστιν παντων κυριοσ

Acts 10:36 The word [which] he sent to the sons of Israel, preaching good news of peace through Jesus (the) Messiah—he is Lord of all—

Acts 18:7 p74vid (Aleph) B* D(2) (E P 945 1739 1891) vg syr(h) geo: > A B(2) D* H L P Psi 049 056 33 614 1241 pc Byz L1178 lat(d.h.p) aeth slav; Chr

18:7 και μεταβασ εκειθεν εισηλθεν εισ οικιαν τινοσ ονοματι [Τιτι<u>ου</u>] Ιουστ<u>ου</u> σεβομεν<u>ου</u> τον θεον ου η οικια ην συνομορουσα τη συναγωγη

Acts 18:7 And he departed there, and went into the house of a certain man named [Titius] Justus, one who worshiped God, whose house was next door to the synagogue.

Acts 21:22 p74 Aleph A (D) E P (Psi) 33 945 1241 (Byz) Lat((ar).c.dem.e.gig.p.ph. ro.w) vg slav; (Heir), (Aug): > B C*vid 614 1739 2495 syr((p).h) sa bo arm(Ms) aeth geo

21:22 τι ουν εστ<u>ιν</u> <u>π</u>αντω<u>σ</u> [δει συνελθε<u>ιν</u> <u>π</u>ληθο<u>σ</u>] ακουσονται οτι εληλυθασ 23 τουτο ουν ποιησον

Acts 21:22 What then? [The multitude must certainly meet.] They will hear that you have come.

Acts 22:9 (D) (E) L P Psi 614 1739 1891 al Byz L1178 lat(e.gig) syr(h) sa aeth slav; Chr: > p74vid Aleph A B H 049 33 181 1175 al lat(ar.c.dem.p.ph.ro.w) vg syr(p) bo arm geo; (Did)

22:9 οι δε συν εμοι οντεσ το μεν φωσ εθεασα**ντο** [και εμφοβοι ε**γενοντο**] την δε φωνην ουκ ηκουσαν του λαλουντοσ μοι

Acts 22:9 "And those who were with me indeed saw the light [and were afraid], but they did not understand the voice of him who spoke to me.

Acts 25:16 H L P 056 88 1241 1611 al Byz lat(gig) vg(cl) syr(p.h**) sa; Chr, Theoph: > p74 Aleph A B C E Psi 33 1175 1739 vg bo; Bas, Thret

25:16 προσ ουσ απεκριθην οτι ουκ εστιν εθοσ Ρωμαιοισ χαριζεσθαι τινα **α**νθρωπο**υ** [εισ **α**πωλεια**υ**] πριν η ο κατηγορουμενοσ κατα προσωπον εχοι τουσ κατηγορουσ τοπον τε απολογιασ λαβοι περι του εγκληματοσ

Acts 25:16 To whom I answered that it is not the custom of the Romans to give up any man [to destruction], before the accused has met the accusers face to face, and has had opportunity to make his defense against the charge.

Romans 1:29 L Psi 049 1735 1874 1962 al Byz Lect (lat(ar.b.o)) vg syr(p.h) arm geo2 slav; (Or(lat1/6)), Bas, GrNy: > (Aleph) B 0172vid 6 1739 1881 L596 sa bo(Mss)) aeth (geo1) (Or(lat2/6))

1:29 πεπληρωμενουσ παση αδικ**ια** [**π**ο**ρνεια**] **π**ονη**ρια** πλεονεξια κακια μεστουσ φθονου φονου εριδοσ δολου κακοηθειασ ψιθυριστασ

Romans 1:29 being filled with all unrighteousness, [sexual immorality] wickedness, covetousness, maliciousness; full of envy, murder, strife, deceit, evil habits, secret slanderers,

Romans 1:31 Aleph(c) C Psi 049 1243 1735 1874 Byz Lect vg syr(p.h) arm geo slav; Or(lat1/2), Bas(1/2), GrNy, Chr: > Aleph* A B D G 1506 1739 lat(ar.b.d.g.mon.o) vg(Mss) sa(Ms) bo; Or(lat1/2), Bas(1/2)

1:31 ασυνετουσ ασυνθετουσ **α**σ**τοργουσ** [**α**σ**π**ον**δουσ**] ανελεημονασ

Romans 1:31 foolish, promise-breakers, heartless, [unforgiving,] unmerciful;

79

Romans 3:22 Aleph(2) D F G K L 049 33 1243 1874 al Byz Lect Lat(ar.b.d.f.g.mon. (o)) vg(cl) syr(p.h) geo slav; Or(lat1/6), Chr: > p40 Aleph* A B C P Psi 81 1739 1881 L60 L598 L599 L617 syr(pal) sa bo arm; Cl, Or(lat5/6), Apo, Did, Cyr

3:22 δικαιοσυνη δε θεου δια πιστεωσ Ιησου Χριστου εισ **παντασ** [και επι **παντασ**] τουσ πιστευοντασ ου γαρ εστιν διαστολη

Romans 3:22 even the righteousness of God through faith in Jesus (the) Messiah to all [and upon all] who believe. For there is no distinction,

Romans 3:22 Aleph(2) D F G K L 049 33 1243 1874 al Byz Lect Lat(ar.b.d.f.g.mon. (o)) vg(cl) syr(p.h) geo slav; Or(lat1/6), Chr: > vg(ww.st) Ambst, Pel, JohnD (Not counted in totals)

3:22 δικαιοσυνη δε θεου δια πιστεωσ Ιησου Χριστου [εισ **παντασ** και] **ε**πι **παντασ**τουσ πιστευοντασ ου γαρ εστιν διαστολη

Romans 3:22 even the righteousness of God through faith in Jesus (the) Messiah [to all and] on all those who believe. For there is no distinction,

Romans 9:28 Aleph(2) D F G K L P Psi 049 33 1243 1874 al Byz Lect Lat(ar.b.d.f.g.o) vg syr(h) arm geo slav; Or(lat), Chr, (Eus1/3): > p46 Aleph* A B 6 1739 1881 pc lat(mon) syr(p) sa bo aeth; Eus2/3, Cyr

9:28 λογον γαρ συντελων και **συντε**μ**γ**ω**ν** [εν δικαιοσυνη οτι λογον **συντε**τμημε**νον**] ποιησει κυριοσ επι τησ γησ

Romans 9:28 (Lit.) For he will fulfill the word and decisively [in righteousness, because the word decisively] will the Lord carry out on the earth.

Romans 10:15 Aleph(2) D K P Psi 049 33 1735 1874 al Byz Lect Lat(b.d.f.g.o) vg syr(p.h) arm geo goth slav(Ms); Mcion, (Ir(lat)), Ad, (Eus), Apo, Chr: > p46 Aleph* A B C 81 1739 1881 lat(ar) sa bo aeth slav(Ms); Cl, Ps-Hipp, Or(gr.lat), Philo-Car

10:15 πωσ δε κηρυξωσιν εαν μη αποσταλωσιν καθωσ γεγραπται ωσ ωραιοι οι ποδεσ **των ευαγγελιζομενων** [ειρηνην **των ευαγγελιζομενων**] τα αγαθα

Romans 10:15 And how will they preach unless they are sent? As it is written: "How beautiful are the feet of those who bring good news [of peace, who bring good news] of good things."

Romans 13:9 Aleph P Psi 048 0150 81 424 1506 al Byz(pt) eight lect lat(ar.b) vg(cl) syr(h.pal) bo arm aeth slav; Or(lat1/6), Chr: > p46vid Avid B D F G Psi 33 1739 1881 al Byz(pt) Lect Lat(d.f.g.o) vg(ww.st) syr(p) sa geo; Cl(1/2), Bas

13:9 το γαρ ου μοιχευσεισ ου φονευσεισ ου κλεψεισ [ου ψευδομαρτυρησεισ] ουκ επιθυμησεισ και ει τισ ετερα εντολη εν τω λογω τουτω ανακεφαλαιουται εν τω αγαπησεισ τον πλησιον σου ωσ σεαυτον

Romans 13:9 For the commandments, "Do not commit adultery," "Do not murder," "Do not steal," ["Do not give false testimony,"] "Do not covet," and whatever other commandments there are, are all summed up in this saying, namely, "You are to love your neighbor as yourself."

Romans 14:6 C(3) L P Psi 049 33 1243 1874 al Byz syr(p.h) arm; Bas, Chr, Thret: > p46 Aleph A B C(2vid) D F G 048 630 1739 1881 pc Latt vg sa bo aeth; Ruf, Ambst, Pel, Aug

14:6 ο φρονων την ημεραν κυριω **φρονει και ο** [μη φρονων την ημεραν κυριω ου **φρονει και ο**] εσθιων κυριω εσθιει ευχαριστει γαρ τω θεω και ο μη εσθιων κυριω ουκ εσθιει και ευχαριστει τω θεω

Romans 14:6 The one who observes the day, observes it to the Lord; [and the one who does not observe the day, he does not observe it to the Lord.] The one who eats, he eats to the Lord; since he gives thanks to God. And the one who does not eat, he does not eat to the Lord, and gives thanks to God.

Romans 14:21 p46vid Aleph(2) B D F G Psi 0209 33vid 614 1881 al Byz Lect Lat(ar.b.d.f.g.o) vg syr(h.(pal)) sa arm geo2 slav; Bas, Chr(1/2.(1/2)): > Aleph* A C 048 81 1739 al lat(r) syr(p) bo aeth geo1; Mcion, Or(gr.lat)

14:21 καλον το μη φαγειν κρεα μηδε πιειν οινον μηδε εν ω ο αδελφοσ σου προσκοπτει [η σκανδαλιζεται η ασθενει] 22 συ πιστιν

Romans 14:21 It is good to not eat meat, drink wine, or do anything by which your brother stumbles, [or is offended, or is made weak].

1 Corinthians 1:14 Aleph(c) (A) C D F G P Psi 0150 (33) 1241 1881 al Byz Lect lat(b.d.f.g.o.r) (lat(ar)) vg(Mss) syr(h) (syr(p.h+) bo(Ms) sa(Mss) aeth geo slav; Or(lat1/2), Chr. [NA28]: > Aleph* B 6 1739 bo(pt) sa(Mss)

1:14 ευχαριστ_ω_ [τω θε_ω_] οτι ουδενα υμων εβαπτισα ει μη Κρισπον και Γαιον

1 Corinthians 1:14 I thank [God] that I baptized none of you, except Crispus and Gaius,

1 Corinthians 1:20 p11 Aleph(2) C(3) D(1) F G L Psi 049 1241 1739(c) 1881 Byz Lat(d.g.r) vg syr(p.h.pal) sa(Ms) bo(pt) arm(Mss) goth; Cl(pt), Epiph(pt): > p46 Aleph* A B C* D* P 33 1739* al sa(Ms) bo(pt); Cl(pt), Epiph(pt)

1:20 που σοφοσ που γραμματευσ που συζητητησ του αιωνοσ τουτου ουχι εμωρανεν ο θεοσ την σοφιαν τ_ου_ κοσμ_ου_ [τουτ_ου_] 21 επειδη

1 Corinthians 1:20 Where is the wise? Where is the scribe? Where is the debater of this world? Hasn't God made foolish the wisdom of [this] world?

1 Corinthians 3:12 Aleph(2) C(3) D L P Psi 049 33 1739 1881 al L249 Byz Lat vg syr sa(Mss) bo arm; Epiph, Bas: > p46 Aleph* A B C* 0289 81 vg(Mss) sa(Mss) bo(Ms) aeth

3:12 ει δε τισ εποικοδομει επι τον θεμελι_ον_ [τουτ_ον_] χρυσον αργυρον λιθουσ τιμιουσ ξυλα χορτον καλαμην

1 Corinthians 3:12 But if anyone builds on [this] foundation with gold, silver, costly stones, wood, hay, or stubble;

1 Corinthians 5:7 Aleph(2) C(3) L P Psi 049 1243 1874 1881 al Byz syr sa bo(Ms); Or: > p11vid p46vid Aleph* A B C*vid F G 33 1175* 1739 pc Latt vg bo; Cl, Or

5:7 εκκαθαρατε την παλαιαν ζυμην ινα ητε νεον φυραμα καθωσ εστε αζυμοι και γαρ το πασχα η_μων_ [υπερ η_μων_] ετυθη Χριστοσ

1 Corinthians 5:7 Purge out the old yeast, that you may be a new lump, even as you are unleavened. For indeed (the) Messiah, our Passover, has been sacrificed [for us].

1 Corinthians 9:20 Aleph A B C D* F G P 0150 33 1739 2495 al Latt(ar.b.d.f.g.o) vg syr(h) sa bo arm; Or(1/2), Chr: > K Psi 614 1241 1881 al Byz Lect syr(p) aeth geo slav; Or(1/2)

9:20 και εγενομην τοισ Ιουδαιοισ ωσ Ιουδαιοσ ινα Ιουδαιουσ κερδησω τοισ υπο νομον ω**σ υπο νομον** [μη ων αυτο**σ υπο νομον**] ινα τους υπο νομον κερδησω

1 Corinthians 9:20 And to the Jews I became as a Jew, that I might gain Jews; to those who are under the law, as under the law, [not being myself under the law,] that I might gain those who are under the law;

2 Corinthians 2:7 p46 Aleph C D G K L P Psi 081 33 1739 1881 al Byz Lect Latt vg syr(h.pal) sa bo: > A B syr(p)

2:7 ωστε τουναντι**ον** [μαλλ**ον**] υμασ χαρισασθαι και παρακαλεσαι μη πωσ τη περισσοτερα λυπη καταποθη ο τοιουτοσ

2 Corinthians 2:7 so that on the contrary you should [rather] forgive him and comfort him, lest by any means such a one should be swallowed up with his excessive sorrow.

2 Corinthians 4:14 Aleph C D F G K L P Psi 075 0150 614 1241 1881 al Byz Lect lat(b.d.f.g.o) vg(Mss) syr(p.h*) bo(Mss) aeth geo2 slav; Chr(1/2): > p46 B (0243 33) 1175* (1739) pc lat(r) vg sa bo(Ms) arm; (Chr(1/2))

4:14 ειδοτεσ οτι ο εγειρασ τ**ον** [κυρι**ον**] Ιησουν και ημασ συν Ιησου εγερει και παραστησει συν υμιν

2 Corinthians 4:14 knowing that he who raised the [Lord] Jesus will raise us also with Jesus, and will present us with you.

2 Corinthians 11:3 p46 p124vid Aleph* B F G 0150 33 1735 1962 pc lat(ar.f.v.r.g.o.r) vg(Mss) syr(h*) sa bo aeth; Heg: > Aleph(2) H K P Psi 049 075 0121 0243 1739 1874 1881 al Byz Lect vg syr(p) arm geo slav; JuCas, Cl, Or(lat), Eus

11:3 φοβουμαι δε μη πωσ ωσ ο οφισ εξηπατησεν Ευαν εν τη πανουργια αυτου φθαρη τα νοηματα υμων απο τησ **απλοτητοσ** [και τησ **αγνοτητοσ**] τησ εισ τον Χριστον

2 Corinthians 11:3 But I am afraid that somehow, as the serpent deceived Eve in his craftiness, so your minds might be corrupted from a sincere [and pure devotion] to (the) Messiah.

2 Corinthians 13:5 Aleph A D(1) G K L P Psi 049 0243 1739 1874 1881 Byz Latt vg (sa bo) arm goth; Chr, Thret: > p46 B D* 33; Cl

13:5 εαυτουσ πειραζετε ει εστε εν τη πιστει εαυτουσ δοκιμαζετε η ουκ επιγινωσκετε εαυτουσ οτι Ιησουσ Χριστοσ εν υμ**ιν** [εστ**ιν**] **ε**ι μητι αδοκιμοι εστε

2 Corinthians 13:5 Test yourselves, whether you are in the faith. Examine yourselves. Or do you not know yourselves, that Jesus (the) Messiah [is] in you?—unless indeed you fail the test.

Galatians 1:15 Aleph A D K L P Psi 049 056 075 33 1241 1739 al Byz Lect lat(d) syr(h+.pal) sa bo arm aeth geo slav; Ir(lat1/2), Or(gr.lat), Eus, Ad, PsAth, Bas. [NA28]: > p46 B F G 0150 2495 lat(ar.b.f.g.o) vg syr(p); Ir(lat1/2.arm), Epiph, Theoph(lat), Thret(2/4)

1:15 οτε δε ευδοκησεν [**ο** θεοσ] **ο** αφορισασ με εκ κοιλιασ μητροσ μου και καλεσασ δια τησ χαριτοσ αυτου

Galatians 1:15 But when [God,] who had set me apart from my mother's womb and called me through his grace, was pleased

Galatians 5:21 A C D F G K L Psi 049 075 0122 0150 88 1739 1881 Byz Lect Latt(ar.b.d.f.g.o) vg syr((p).h) bo aeth arm geo2 goth slav; Ps-Cl, Bas, Chr, Theo(lat): > p46 Aleph B P 33 81 218 six lect sa geo1 Mcion, Ir(lat), Cl, Or(lat)

5:21 **φθονοι** [**φονοι**] μεθαι κωμοι και τα ομοια τουτοισ α προλεγω υμιν καθωσ προειπον οτι οι τα τοιαυτα πρασσοντεσ βασιλειαν θεου ου κληρονομησουσιν

Galatians 5:21 envy, [murders,] drunkenness, orgies, and things like these, about which I warn you, as I warned you before, that those who practice such things will not inherit the Kingdom of God.

Ephesians 5:30 Aleph(2) D F G (K) P Psi 0278 0285vid 614 1241 1739mg al Byz Lect Lat(ar.b.d.f.g.mon.o) vg syr((p).h) arm geo slav; Ir(gr.lat), Chr, Theod(lat): > p46 Aleph* A B 048 33 81 1739* 1881 pc L422 lat(s) sa bo aeth; Or(lat), Meth

5:30 οτι μελη εσμεν του σωματοσ **αυτου** [εκ τησ σαρκοσ αυτου και εκ των οστεων **αυτου**] 31 αντι τουτου

Ephesians 5:30 because we are members of his body, [of his flesh and of his bones].

Philippians 3:12 p46 p61 Aleph A Psi 075 1241 1739 al Byz Lect (lat(ar)) (vg) syr(h(mg)) bo(pt) arm geo slav; Chr(1/2). [NA28]: > B D* F G 33 lat(b.d.g.o) sa; Cl, Or(lat)

3:12 ουχ οτι ηδη ελαβον η ηδη τετελειωμαι διωκω δε ει και καταλαβω εφ ω και κατελημφθην υπο Χριστ**ου** [Ιησ**ου**] 13 αδελφοι

Philippians 3:12 Not that I have already obtained, or am already made perfect; but I press on, if it is so that I may take hold of that for which also I was taken hold of by Messiah [Jesus].

Philippians 3:16 Aleph(2) K P Psi 075 424* 2464 al Byz Lect (vg) syr(p.h) aeth(pp); Bas, Chr, Theod(lat): > p16 p46 Aleph* A B Ivid 0150 6 33 1739 lat(b) (sa(Mss)) bo aeth; (TheoA)

3:16 πλην εισ ο εφθασαμεν **τω** **αυτ**ω στοιχ**ειν** [κανονι **το** **αυτ**ο φρον**ειν**] 17 συμμιμηται μου

Philippians 3:16 Nevertheless, to what we have attained, let us walk by the same [rule, being of the same mind].

Colossians 1:20 p46 Aleph A C Psi 048 0150 33 1243 1735 al Byz Lect syr(p.h) bo geo slav; Chr(1/2), Theod(lat), Cyr(1/5) [NA28]: > B D* F G I L 075 1739 1874 1881 al four lect Latt(ar.b.d.f.g.mon.o) vg syr(pal) sa aeth arm; Or, Did, Chr(1/2), Cyr(4/5)

1:20 και δι αυτου αποκαταλλαξαι τα παντα εισ αυτον ειρηνοποιησασ δια του αιματοσ του σταυρου **αυτου** [δι **αυτου**] ειτε τα επι τησ γησ ειτε τα εν τοισ ουρανοισ

Colossians 1:20 and through him to reconcile all things to himself, making peace through the blood of his cross [through him], whether things on the earth or things in heaven.

Colossians 2:7 B D(2) H K L 049 0278 945 1505 1735 al Byz Lect lat((ar).mon.(o)) vg(Ms) syr(p.h) sa(Ms) bo geo2; Chr, Theod(lat): > Aleph* A C H* Ivid 075 0150 0208 33 1739 1881 pc vg(st.ww) sa(Mss) aeth geo1 slav

2:7 ερριζωμενοι και εποικοδομουμενοι εν αυτω και βεβαιουμενοι τη πιστει καθωσ εδιδαχθητε περισσευοντεσ [**εν** αυτη] **εν** ευχαριστια

Colossians 2:7 rooted and built up in him, and established in the faith, even as you were taught, abounding [in it] with thanksgiving.

1 Thessalonians 5:21 Aleph(c) B D G K P Psi 1241 1739 1881 2495 Byz(pt) Lat vg syr(h) bo(Mss) sa: > Aleph* A 33 614 630 al Byz(pt) Lect lat(f) syr(p.pal) bo(Mss); Did

5:21 παντα [**δε**] **δ**οκιμαζετε το καλον κατεχετε

1 Thessalonians 5:21 [but] test all things; hold firmly that which is good.

1 Thessalonians 5:27 p46vid Aleph(2) A K P Psi 075 0150 33 1739 1881 al Byz Lect lat(ar) vg syr(p.h.pal) bo arm (aeth) geo2; Chr, Theod(lat): > Aleph* B D F G 0278 436 2464 lat(b.d.f.g.mon.o) sa geo1 slav; Ambst, Cass

5:27 ενορκιζω υμασ τον κυριον αναγνωσθηναι την επιστολην πασιν τ**οισ** [**α**γι**οισ**] **α**δελφοισ

1 Thessalonians 5:27 I solemnly command you by the Lord that this letter be read to all the [holy] brothers.

2 Thessalonians 2:8 Aleph A D* F G P Psi 075 0150 33 81 1241 al Latt((ar).b.d.f.g.mon.o) vg syr(p.h) sa bo arm aeth slav; Ir(lat), Hipp, Or(gr3/4. lat), Ath, CyrJ, Did, Chr, Theo(lat). [NA28]: > B D(2) K 614 1739 1881 al Byz Lect bo(Ms) geo; Ir(gr), Jos, Mac/Sym, Thret(1/2)

2:8 και τοτε αποκαλυφθησεται ο ανομοσ ον ο κυριο**σ** [Ιησου**σ**] ανελει τω πνευματι του στοματοσ αυτου και καταργησει τη επιφανεια τησ παρουσιασ αυτου

2 Thessalonians 2:8 And then the lawless one will be revealed, whom the Lord [Jesus] will kill with the breath of his mouth, and destroy by the manifestation of his coming;

1 Timothy 5:16 D K L Psi 075 0150 945 1900 1962 al Byz Lect lat(ar.b.d.o) vg(Mss) syr(p.h) slav; Chr: > Aleph A C F G P 048 33 1739 1881 lat(mon) vg sa bo; Ath

5:16 ει τισ [**πιστ**οσ η] **πιστ**η εχει χηρασ επαρκειτω αυταισ και μη βαρεισθω η εκκλησια ινα ταισ οντωσ χηραισ επαρκεση

1 Timothy 5:16 If any [believing man or] believing woman has widows, let them assist them, and do not let the church be burdened; that it might help those widows who are truly in need.

2 Timothy 3:6 A 1245 1505 syr(h); Thret: > Aleph D F G Psi 33 1739 1874 al Byz vg syr(p)

3:6 εκ τουτων γαρ εισιν οι ενδυνοντεσ εισ τασ οικιασ και αιχμαλωτιζοντεσ γυναικαρια σεσωρευμενα αμαρτιαισ αγομενα επιθυμι**αισ** [και ηδον**αισ**] ποικιλαισ

2 Timothy 3:6 For among them are those who creep into households and take captive weak-willed women weighed down with sins, led away by various passions [and pleasures],

Hebrews 7:21 Aleph(2) A D Psi 075 1241 1739 1881 al Byz Lect lat(ar.d) vg(Mss) syr(p.h) bo(pt) aeth geo slav; Eus, Chr, Thret: > p46 (Aleph*) B C 0150 33 81 2464 pc lat(b.comp.m.r) vg syr(pal) sa bo(pt) arm

7:21–22 ο δε μετα ορκωμοσιασ δια του λεγοντοσ προσ αυτον ωμοσεν κυριοσ και ου μεταμεληθησεται συ ιερευσ εισ τον αιωνα [**κατα τ**ην ταξιν μελχισεδεκ] 22 **κατα τ**οσουτο και κρειττονοσ διαθηκησ γεγονεν εγγυοσ ιησουσ

Hebrews 7:21 for they indeed have been made priests without an oath, but he with an oath by him that says of him, "The Lord swore and will not change his mind, 'You are a priest forever, [according to the order of Melchizedek].'"

Hebrews 9:19 Aleph* A C P 33 614 630 al Byz (om. των by hpgr) Lect Lat vg sa(Mss) arm geo slav. [NA28]: > p46 Aleph(2) K L Psi 0150 1241 1739 1881 pc syr((p).h.pal); Chr

9:19 ληληθεισησ γαρ πασησ εντολησ κατα τον νομον υπο Μωυσεωσ παντι τω λαω λαβων το αιμα τ_ων_ μοσχ_ων_ [και τ_ων_ τραγ_ων_] μετα υδατοσ και εριου κοκκινου και υσσωπου αυτο τε το βιβλιον και παντα τον λαον ερραντισεν

Hebrews 9:19 For when every commandment had been spoken by Moses to all the people according to the Law, he took the blood of the calves [and the goats], with water and scarlet wool and hyssop, and sprinkled both the book itself and all the people,

Hebrews 11:11 p46 D*.b (P Psi 075 0150 81 1739 1881) al Lat(ar.b.comp.d.z) vg syr(p.h) (sa) (bo) (arm) (aeth) geo slav: > p13vid Aleph A D(2) K 33 424* 630 pc Byz Lect; Chr

11:11 πιστει και αυτη Σαρ_ρα_ [στει_ρα_] δυναμιν εισ καταβολην σπερματοσ ελαβεν και παρα καιρον ηλικιασ επει πιστον ηγησατο τον επαγγειλαμενον

Hebrews 11:11 By faith, even [barren] Sarah herself received power to conceive when she was past age, and gave birth, since she considered him faithful who had promised.

Hebrews 11:37 p13vid (Aleph) A D(2) K (P) (048) 075 (33) 1739 1881 al Byz Lect Lat(ar.b.comp.(d).z) vg (syr(h)) (syr(pal)) bo arm (geo) slav; Or(gr4/5.lat1/2), Acac, Chr, (Hier): > p46 1241 lect syr(p) (sa) aeth; Or(gr1/5.lat1/2), Eus, (Did), Nil

11:37 ελιθασθησαν **επρισθησαν** [επειρα**σθησαν**] εν φονω μαχαιρησ απεθανον περιηλθον εν μηλωταισ εν αιγειοισ δερμασιν υστερουμενοι θλιβομενοι κακουχουμενοι

Hebrews 11:37 They were stoned, they were sawed apart, [they were tempted,] they were killed with the sword; they went around in sheepskins and goatskins; being destitute, afflicted, mistreated

James 4:4 Aleph(2) K L P Psi 049 056 0142 945 1241 1735 al Byz Lect syr(h*) geo(Mss) slav: > p100 Aleph* A B 33 1243 1739 pc Latt(ar.ff.s.t) vg syr(p.h) sa bo arm aeth geo(Mss); Aug

δαπανησητε 4:4 [**μοιχ**οι και] **μοιχ**αλιδεσ ουκ οιδατε οτι η φιλια του κοσμου εχθρα του θεου εστιν οσ εαν ουν βουληθη φιλοσ ειναι του κοσμου εχθροσ του θεου καθισταται

James 4:4 [Adulterers and] adulteresses, do you not know that friendship with the world is hostility toward God? Therefore whoever wants to be a friend of the world makes himself an enemy of God.

1Peter 1:22 p72 Aleph* C K P Psi 33 1739 1881 al Byz Lect lat(t) vg(Mss) syr(p.h) sa bo (arm) slav: > A B 1852 lat(ar) vg geo; Var

1:22 τασ ψυχασ υμων ηγνικοτεσ εν τη υπακοη τησ αληθειασ εισ φιλαδελφιαν ανυποκριτον εκ [**καθαρασ**] **κα**ρδι**ασ** αλληλουσ αγαπησατε εκτενωσ

1 Peter 1:22 Seeing you have purified your souls in your obedience to the truth in sincere brotherly affection, love one another from a [pure] heart fervently:

1Peter 4:14 Aleph(1) K L P S (Psi) 1 1563 2191 al Byz L590 lat(ar.q.t.z) vg(ww) syr(h*) sa(Mss) (bo(Ms)) slav; (Cyp), Aug: > p72 Aleph A B 049 33 1739 al vg(cl. st) syr(p.h) sa(Ms) bo arm aeth geo; Cl, Thret, Cyr

4:14 ει ονειδιζεσθε εν ονοματι Χριστου μακαριοι οτι το τησ δοξησ και το του θεου πνευμα εφ **υμασ** αναπαυ**εται** [κατα μεν αυτουσ βλασφημειται κατα δε **υμασ** δοξα**ζεται**] 15 μη

1 Peter 4:14 If you are insulted for the name of Messiah, you are blessed; because the Spirit of glory and of God rests on you. [On their part he is blasphemed, but on your part he is glorified.]

2Peter 2:6 Aleph A C(2) K Psi 33 614 2495 al Byz Lect Lat(ar.h.z) vg syr(ph.h) sa arm aeth geo slav: > p72 B C* 1175 1739 pc L596 bo

2:6 και πολεισ Σοδομων και Γομορρασ τεφρωσασ [**κατ**αστροφη] **κατ**εκρινεν υποδειγμα μελλοντων ασεβειν τεθεικωσ

2 Peter 2:6 and turning the cities of Sodom and Gomorrah [to ashes], condemned them to destruction, having made them an example of what is going to happen to the ungodly;

Jude 1:25 Aleph A(vid) B C Psi 945 1739 al vg.: > 049 218 1243 1448 al Byz

1:25 μονω θεω σωτηρι **ημων** [δια Ιησου Χριστου του κυριου **ημων**] δοξα μεγαλωσυνη κρατοσ και εξουσια προ παντοσ του αιωνοσ και νυν και εισ παντασ τουσ αιωνασ αμην

Jude 1:25 to the only God our Savior, [through Jesus (the) Messiah our Lord,] be glory and majesty, dominion and power, both now and forever. Amen.

Revelation 2:13 Aleph P (046) 1611 1854 2050 2814 Byz(A,B,C) (Byz(K)) lat(gig.t) (lat syr(h)): > A C 2053 2344 lat(ar) vg syr(ph) sa bo

2:13 οιδα που κατοικεισ οπου ο θρονοσ του σατανα και κρατεισ το ονομα μου και ουκ ηρνησω την πιστιν μου και εν ταισ ημερ**αισ** [εν **αισ**] Αντιπασ ο μαρτυσ μου ο πιστοσ μου οσ απεκτανθη παρ υμιν οπου ο σατανασ κατοικει

Revelation 2:13 "I know where you dwell, where Satan's throne is. You hold firmly to my name, and did not deny my faith even in the days [in which] Antipas was my witness, my faithful one, who was killed among you, where Satan dwells.

Revelation 5:3 046 1006 1841 2351 Byz(K) syr(p.h): > 1854 2814 2845 Byz(A) vg

5:3 και ουδεισ εδυνατο εν τω ουρ**ανω** [**ανω**] ουδε επι τησ γησ ουδε υποκατω τησ γησ ανοιξαι το βιβλιον ουτε βλεπειν αυτο

Revelation 5:3 No one in heaven [above], or on the earth, or under the earth, was able to open the scroll, or to look in it.

Revelation 5:5 Aleph 2344 2814 vg(cl) syr(ph) arm(Mss); Cyp, Apr, And: > A 69 1006 1854 al Byz syr(p) vg

5:5 και εισ εκ των πρεσβυτερων λεγει μοι μη κλαιε ιδου ενικησεν ο λεων ο εκ τησ φυλησ Ιουδα η ριζα Δαυιδ ανοιξαι το βιβλιον κ**αι** [λυσ**αι**] τασ επτα σφραγιδασ αυτου

Revelation 5:5 And one of the elders said to me, "Do not weep. Look, the Lion who is of the tribe of Judah, the Root of David, has overcome so that he can open the scroll and [loose] its seven seals."

Revelation 5:9 94 2050 2344 vg syr arm; Hipp, Cyp: > A 2814 Byz aeth

5:9 και αδουσιν ωδην καινην λεγοντεσ αξιοσ ει λαβειν το βιβλιον και ανοιξαι τασ σφραγιδασ αυτου οτι εσφαγησ και ηγορασ**ασ** [ημ**ασ**] τω θεω εν τω αιματι σου εκ πασησ φυλησ και γλωσσησ και λαου και εθνουσ

Revelation 5:9 They sang a new song, saying, "You are worthy to take the scroll, and to open its seals: for you were killed, and redeemed [us] for God with your blood, out of every tribe, language, people, and nation,

Revelation 6:9 Aleph P 1841 2344 Byz(A) sa bo aeth(ro) arm: > A C 69 1006 1854 2814 Byz(K) vg syr aeth(pp); Cl

6:9 και οτε ηνοιξεν την πεμπτην σφραγιδα ειδον υποκατω του θυσιαστηριου τασ ψυχασ [**των** ανθρωπων] **των** εσφαγμενων δια τον λογον του θεου και δια την μαρτυριαν ην ειχον

Revelation 6:9 When he opened the fifth seal, I saw underneath the altar the souls of [people] who had been killed for the Word of God, and for the testimony which they had.

Revelation 7:1 Aleph 046 1611 2329 2344 2814 al Byz(K) syr(ph) arm aeth; Bea: > A C 1006 1854 2053 pc Latt vg

6:17 ...και τισ δυναται σταθην**αι** 7:1 [κ**αι**] μετα τουτο ειδον τεσσαρασ αγγελουσ εστωτασ επι τασ τεσσαρασ γωνιασ τησ γησ κρατουντασ τουσ τεσσαρασ ανεμουσ τησ γησ ινα μη πνεη ανεμοσ επι τησ γησ μητε επι τησ θαλασσησ μητε επι παν δενδρον

Revelation 7:1 [And] after this, I saw four angels standing at the four corners of the earth, holding the four winds of the earth, so that no wind would blow on the earth, or on the sea, or on any tree.

Revelation 8:7 p115vid Aleph A 35 424 1006 al Byz vg syr : > 1854 2814 [TR]

8:7 και ο πρωτοσ εσαλπισεν και εγενετο χαλαζα και πυρ μεμιγμενα εν αιματι και εβληθη εισ την γην **και το τριτον** [τησ γησ κατεκαη **και το τριτον**] **τ**ων δενδρων κατεκαη και πασ χορτοσ χλωροσ κατεκαη

Revelation 8:7 And the first sounded, and there followed hail and fire, mixed with blood, and they were thrown to the earth. And one third [of the earth was burnt up, and one third] of the trees were burnt up, and all green grass was burnt up.

Revelation 9:4 046 1006 2329 2814 al Byz(K) vg(ww) syr arm aeth; Tyc Prim: > Aleph A P 1854 lat(ar.gig) vg(st)

9:4 και ερρεθη αυταισ ινα μη αδικησουσιν τον χορτον τησ γησ ουδε παν χλωρον ουδε παν δενδρον ει μη τους ανθρωπουσ οιτινεσ ουκ εχουσιν την σφραγιδα του θεου επι των μετωπ**ων** [αυτ**ων**] 5 και

Revelation 9:4 They were told that they should not hurt the grass of the earth, neither any green thing, neither any tree, but only those people who do not have God's seal on [their] foreheads.

Revelation 9:13 (P) (046) 1006 1854 2814 al Byz lat vg(cl) syr(ph); And. [NA28]: > p47 Aleph(1) A 0207 1611 2053 2344 Byz(A) lat(ar.gig) vg(ww.st) syr(h) sa(Ms) bo aeth

9:13 και ο εκτοσ αγγελοσ εσαλπισεν και ηκουσα φωνην μιαν εκ τ**ων** [τεσσαρ**ων**] κερατων του θυσιαστηριου του χρυσου του ενωπιον του θεου

Revelation 9:13 The sixth angel sounded. I heard a voice from the [four] horns of the golden altar which is before God,

Revelation 13:10 p47vid (Aleph) C P 046 051txt 2053 2329 2814 pc Byz(A) lat; Ir(lat): > A Byz(K) vg(ww.st); Ps-Ambr

13:10 ει τισ εισ αιχμαλωσιαν εισ αιχμαλωσιαν υπαγει ει τισ εν μαχαιρη αποκτεν**ει** [δ**ει**] αυτον εν μαχαιρη αποκτανθηναι ωδε εστιν η υπομονη και η πιστισ των αγιων

Revelation 13:10 If anyone is to go into captivity, he will go into captivity. If anyone is to be killed with the sword, he [must] be killed with the sword. Here is the endurance and the faith of the saints.

Revelation 18:2 2329 Byz(B(pt)) lat(gig) syr(h) (sa) (aeth Ms) (arm); (Hipp); (Prim). [NA28]: > Aleph C 051 1006 2053 2814 Byz(K.C) Byz(B(pt)) lat(ar) vg bo (aeth Ms); And, Bea

18:2 και εκραξεν εν ισχυρα φωνη λεγων επεσεν επεσεν Βαβυλων η μεγαλη και εγενετο κατοικητηριον δαιμονιων και φυλακη παντοσ πνευματοσ ακαθαρτου και φυλακη παντοσ ορνε**ου ακαθαρτου [και** φυλακη παντοσ θηρι**ου ακαθαρτου] και** μεμισημενου

Revelation 18:2 He shouted with a mighty voice, saying, "Fallen, fallen is Babylon the great, and she has become a habitation of demons, a prison of every unclean spirit, and a prison of every unclean bird, [and a prison of every unclean beast] and detestable.

Revelation 21:4 Aleph(1) 205 209 1854 2814 Byz lat(ar) vg(cl.ww) syr(h) sa (bo) arm; Ir(lat). [NA28]: > Aleph* A P 051supp 1006 1611 2329 pc; And

21:4 και εξαλειψει παν δακρυον εκ των οφθαλμων αυτων και ο θανατοσ ουκ εσται ετι ουτε πενθοσ ουτε κραυγη ουτε πονοσ ουκ εσται ε**τι [οτι]** τα πρωτα απηλθαν

Revelation 21:4 And he will wipe away every tear from their eyes, and death will be no more, nor will there be mourning, nor crying, nor pain, anymore, [for] the first things have passed away."

Conclusion

Text critical examples of haplography in Biblical manuscripts published in the literature as well as examples identified from primary research were compiled into a list numbering 374 examples, and the full meaning and intent of the passages can now be seen once the missing text has been restored. Of particular note is the tremendous amount of text that has been recovered with comparison of manuscripts of the Greek Septuagint (LXX), translated between the 3rd and 2nd centuries BC in Egypt.

The Dead Sea Scrolls,[1] Syriac Peshitta,[2] Targum[3] and Latin Vulgate[4] also contributed to the recovery of words that had dropped out of the Masoretic text (MT). In a few instances, two or more manuscripts were required to determine the text that was lost.[5]

From the list of examples of haplography the type of letter involvement and frequency were tabulated. For the New Testament (NT), a total of 117 examples of haplography were found in several Greek NT editions. The Nestle-Aland 28th Greek NT edition (NA28) was involved with 115, and this edition was used for analysis in Table 1. Included in the 115 examples are 44 that are bracketed in the NA28 Greek NT edition as uncertain but are here identified as missing in manuscripts due to haplography.

Table 1: Haplography Involvement and Frequency

	OT		NT	
Examples	256		117	
		%		%
1 word+	69	26.8	41	35.7
homoiologon	7	2.7	0	0.0
1 h.a.	41	16.0	4	3.5
1 h.a. (sc)	1	0.4	0	0.0
1 h.t.	27	10.5	5	4.3
1 h.t. (sc)	6	2.3	0	0.0
2+ h.a.	50	19.5	11	9.6
2+ h.a. (sc)	4	1.6	0	0.0
2+ h.t.	45	17.5	52	45.2
2+ h.t. (sc)	7	2.7	0	0.0
aural	0	0.0	1	0.9
overbar h.t.	0	0.0	1	0.9
Total	256	100.0	115	100.0

h.a. : homoioarcton
h.t. : homoioteleuton
sc: sight confusion

The most significant causes of haplography in the Old Testament (OT) involved whole-word skips (29.6%),[6] followed by two-letter or more homoioarcton (19.5%).

In the NA28 edition the primary cause of haplography was two-letter or more homoioteleuton (45.2%), followed by whole-word involvement (35.7%). Cases of two-letter or more homoioarcton were less in the Greek NT (9.6%) when compared to the Hebrew OT (19.5%).

Since many of the examples in the haplography list are taken from the literature and have been commented on, only a few of particular interest will be noted.

In the first chapter of Genesis, the creation account, sixteen Hebrew words had dropped out of MT from scribal haplography by homoioarcton.[7] Also of interest are three words that fell out of Exodus 20:12, one of the ten commandments, from a five-letter homoioteleuton.[8]

The MT books of 1 & 2 Samuel have been especially noted by text critics as having lost a considerable amount of text from haplography.[9] In this study the words lost in the two books total 439, which should be viewed as a conservative estimate. The top five are: 1Samuel 305, Judges 135, 2Samuel 134, 1Kings 103, Genesis 103.

Also of interest is Psalm 67:4 where a single LXX manuscript, codex Sinaiticus (c. 330-360 AD), preserves 3 words that fell out from an early scribal haplography.[10] Some copyist haplography in MT was found to impact NT quotes, including Exodus 2:14, Deuteronomy 32:43, Psalm 118:6 and Isaiah 40:5. For a more extensive list, see Appendix.

In this comparison of the MT with other manuscripts the total Hebrew words that fell out of MT between the years 1450 BC and 1009 AD from copyist haplography number 1109, or 4274 letters.

For the New Testament, of particular interest was the finding that three complete verses dropped out of NA28 from scribal haplography, viz Mark 11:26, 15:28 and Luke 23:17, but are present in the 1516 Greek NT text of Erasmus and the 1611 King James Bible (KJB). Also of note are OT quotes with some text lacking in NA28, e.g., Matthew 2:18, Luke 4:18, Romans 9:28 and 10:15, the cause of which can be traced to early haplography.

The total words lost from scribal haplography in NA28, a modern Greek NT, number 247. To this can be added 100 words which are bracketed by the NA28 editors and are missing in many manuscripts but whose absence can be explained from haplography.[11] Tested against the same 117 examples in the list, the SBL Greek New Testament has lost 259 words, with 7 bracketed. The earliest complete New Testament manuscript, codex Sinaiticus, has lost 281 words.

The 1516 Greek NT edition of Desiderius Erasmus was also compared to the list, and a total of 39 words were identified as having dropped out from scribal haplography.[12] The Byzantine Majority text according to Robinson-Pierpont is a few less, with 36 words.

Table 2: Haplography in New Testament Editions

	Year	Words Lost	Words Bracketed
Codex Sinaiticus	c. 350	281	
Jerome-Vulgate	c. 400	115	
Erasmus	1516	39	
Tischendorf	1872	286	17
Westcott-Hort	1881	306	40
Robinson-Pierpont	2005	36	
SBL	2010	259	7
NA28	2012	247	100

The total amount of words lost from copyist haplography in a Bible with an uncorrected Masoretic text and a modern Greek NT is 1356. For a Bible with a NT based on the KJB Greek text, the total words missing from haplography number 1148.

Since this study was not exhaustive, further study of the Biblical manuscripts is suggested to identify any additional examples of text lost due to copyist oversight.

While a few Bibles have some of the words in the list restored that were lost during the era of hand copying, a considerable amount of text is left to restore to the Bible. Let's join in earnest prayer that God would raise up Bible editors and translators all over the world whose desire is to restore God's precious words.

NOTES

1. Exo 40:18, Num 4:7, 1Sam 10:27-11:1a, 1Sam 21:4, 2Sam 24:16, 1Kgs 8:16, Isa 16:7, Joe 2:19.
2. 1Kgs 7:20, 2Kgs 9:27, Jer 5:19
3. 1Chr 6:15, 2Chr 16:14
4. 1Sam 24:10, Dan 5:3
5. E.g., Deu 32:43, 1Kgs 8:16
6. 69 + 7 homoiologon = 29.6%.
7. Freedman and Miano, 278-79.
8. Freedman and Overton, 106; G. J. Steyn, A Comparison of the Septuagint Textual Form, in XIV Congress of the International Organization for Septuagint and Cognate Studies, 611.
9. R. W. Klein, 1 Samuel, Word Biblical Commentary, xxvi.
10. H. J. Kraus, Psalmen, Biblischer Kommentar Altes Testament (1978), 621.
11. For NA28, the 115 are comprised of 71 unbracketed examples (= 247 Greek words lost) + 44 bracketed examples (= 100 Greek words bracketed). Statistics for the 71 unbracketed examples: 1 word+ = 38.0%, 2+ end (h.t.) = 45.1%, 2+ begin (h.a.) = 11.3%, 1 end (h.t.) = 4.2%, 1 begin (h.a.) = 1.4%.
12. The 1516 Greek text of Erasmus of the verses under examination in this study is identical to the 1611 Greek text of the KJB as reconstructed by F. H. A. Scrivener in 1894.

Appendix

Haplography, Misreadings and Edits in MT Impacting NT Quotes

Genesis 2:24 LXX Syr Tg Ms Vg (sight confusion in PH)
באשתו והיו [שניהם] לבשר אחד:

Genesis 2:24 Therefore a man will leave his father and his mother, and will join with his wife, and the **two** will be one flesh.

Comments: The LXX and other manuscripts and Matthew 19:5 GNT have "two," which is lacking in MT, apparently from homoioteleuton by sight confusion in Paleo-Hebrew: whyw-nyhm.

Genesis 11:13 LXX(H)
שנים וארבע מאות שנה ויולד בנים ובנות [ויחי קינן שלשים
שנה ומאת שנה ויולד את ושלח ויחי קינן אחרי הולידו את שלח
שלשים שנים ושלש מאות שנה ויולד בנים ובנית] וישלח

Genesis 11:13 And Arpachshad lived after he became the father of **Kenan thirty and four hundred years, and fathered sons and daughters. And Kenan lived thirty and a hundred years, and became the father of Shelah. And Kenan lived after he had become the father of Shelah thirty years and three hundred years, and fathered sons and daughters.**

Comments: The LXX and Luke 3:36 GNT have information about Kenan son of Arpachshad, while the MT lacks it. When the MT is compared with the Hebrew Vorlage of the LXX it can be seen that a haplography in the MT text stream took place involving a five word string to its next occurrence, removing 23 Hebrew words. With the loss of text dealing with the birth of Shelah, and vv. 14-15 pointing to v. 13 for his birth, several scribal adjustments followed: 1) a change of "Kenan" to "Shelah" in 11:12 and 13, 2) a change of "thirty" to "three" in 11:13 for Shelah, and 3) removal of "Kenan" from 10:24 (although a simultaneous haplography is possible there) and 1Chronicles 1:18 and 24. That secondary scribal adjustments sometimes occurred following loss of text from haplography is well documented.

Genesis 15:6 LXX(H)
[ויאמן אברם באלהים] ויחשבה לו צדקה

Genesis 15:6 And **Abram** believed **God**, and it was credited to him as righteousness.

Comments: The LXX and Romans 4:3, etc, GNT read the above while MT reads "And he believed the LORD, and he credited it to him." A phenomena in MT and other manuscripts is the occasional scribal change of divine names. The LXX and GNT provide witness that the original divine name in this verse was "God."

Genesis 47:31 LXX(H)
על ראש [הַמַּטֶּה]:

Genesis 47:31 He said, "Swear to me," and he swore to him. And Israel bowed himself, leaning on the top of his **staff**.

Comments: The LXX and Hebrews 11:21 GNT read rabdou = matteh הַמַּטֶּה "staff" while MT reads mittah הַמִּטָּה "bed," a difference in scribal vocalization of the consonantal text.

Exodus 1:5 DSS LXX
ויעקב [חמש] ושבעים נפש

Exodus 1:5 All the souls who came out of Jacob's body were seventy-**five**, and Joseph was in Egypt already.

Comments: Acts 7:14 GNT reads "seventy-five" and it is not clear whether the quote is from Genesis 46:27 or Exodus 1:5. In Genesis 46:27 LXX reads "seventy-five," while Exodus 1:5 in DSS (2 Mss) and LXX read "seventy-five." MT reads "seventy" in both passages. It is possible that a scribe in the MT text stream harmonized the numbers in Genesis 46:27 and Exodus 1:5 to the reading of "seventy" found in Deuteronomy 10:22.

Exodus 2:14 LXX(H)
הרגת [אֶתְמוֹל] אֵת המצרי

Exodus 2:14 He said, "Who made you a prince and a judge over us? Do you plan to kill me, as you killed the Egyptian **yesterday**?" Moses was afraid, and said, "Surely this thing is known."

Comments: The LXX and Acts 7:28 GNT have "yesterday" while MT lacks the word, apparently from a two letter homoioarcton.

Exodus 20:12 Nash Pap. LXX(H)
אמל לְמַעַן [ייטב לך וּלְמַעַן] יארכון

Exodus 20:12 "Honor your father and your mother, **that it may be well with you**, that your days may be long in the land which the LORD your God gives you.

Comments: The Nash Papyrus, LXX and Ephesians 6:3 GNT have "that it may be well with you" while MT lacks the words, apparently from homoioteleuton.

Deuteronomy 8:3 LXX(H)
מוצא פי [אלהים] יחיה האדם

Deuteronomy 8:3 He humbled you, and allowed you to be hungry, and fed you with manna, which you did not know, neither did your fathers know; that he might make you know that man does not live by bread alone, but man lives by everything that proceeds out of the mouth of **God** shall man live.

Comments: The LXX and Matthew 4:4 GNT read "God" while MT reads "the LORD." Cf. comments on Genesis 15:6.

Deuteronomy 19:15 LXX(H)
עדים יקום [כָּל] דָּבָר

Deuteronomy 19:15 One witness shall not rise up against a man for any iniquity, or for any sin, in any sin that he sins: at the mouth of two witnesses, or at the mouth of three witnesses, shall **every** word be established.

Comments: The LXX and Matthew 18:16 GNT have the word "every" while MT lacks this word, possibly from homoioarcton by sight confusion in a square script: k-d.

Deuteronomy 32:43 DSS+LXX(H)
[הרנינו] שמים עמו והשתחוו לו כל מלאכי אלהים] הרנינו
גוים עמו ויחזקו לו כל מלאכי אלהים כי דם בניו יקום ונקם
ונקם ישיב לצריו ולמשנאיו ישלם ויכפר אדמת עמו

Deuteronomy 32:43 Rejoice, O heavens, with him, and let all the angels of God worship him. Rejoice, O nations, with his people, and let all the angels of God strengthen themselves in him. For he will avenge the blood of his sons, and he will avenge and recompense justice to his enemies, and he will recompense them that hate him, and he will cleanse the land for his people.

Comments: The LXX, DSS and Hebrews 1:6 GNT (in part) have "Rejoice, O heavens, with him, and let all the angels of God worship him" while MT lacks the words, apparently from a six letter scribal haplography. The causes for the loss of the other words in this verse in MT are generally unknown.

Psalm 8:2 LXX(H)
וינקים יסדת [עןֹ] למען צורריך

Psalm 8:2 From the lips of babes and infants you have ordained **praise**, because of your adversaries, that you might silence the enemy and the avenger.

Comments: The LXX and Matthew 21:16 GNT read ainon "praise" = עןֹ while MT reads עֹז "strength," a nun(f)-zayin confusion in a square script. " Cf. BDB 777; Lane 6: 2293; T. F. McDaniel, Problem Quotations, pp.10-11.

Psalm 8:5 LXX(H)
ותחסרהו מעט [מלאכים] וכבוד והדר

Psalm 8:5 For you have made him a little lower than the **angels**, and you have crowned him with glory and honor.

Comments: The LXX and Hebrews 2:7 GNT read aggelous "angels" = מלאכים while MT reads מֵאֱלֹהִים "from God," a scribal misreading possibly involving a metathesis of lamed and aleph.

Psalm 10:7 LXX(H)
פיהו מלא [ומררות] ותך תחת

Psalm 10:7 His mouth is full of cursing **and bitterness** and oppression. Under his tongue is mischief and iniquity.

Comments: The LXX and Romans 3:14 GNT read pikrias "bitterness" = ומררות while MT reads ומרמות "deceit," a scribal misreading with a one letter difference.

Psalm 16:9 LXX(H)
לבי ויגל [לשוני] אף בשרי

Psalm 16:9 Therefore my heart is glad, and my **tongue** rejoices. My body shall also dwell in safety.

Comments: The LXX and Acts 2:26 GNT read glossa "tongue" = לשוני while MT reads כבודי "glory." While both words contain five letters, two being the same in the same position, and two others somewhat similar in square script, the words are apparently not easily confused and it may be that the MT scroll was damaged and very difficult to read.

Psalm 19:4 LXX(H) Symmachus Vg Jerome
הארץ יצא [קולם] ובקצה

Psalm 19:4 Their **voice** has gone out through all the earth, their words to the end of the world. In them he has set a tent for the sun,

Comments: The LXX and Romans 10:18 GNT read phthoggos "voice" = קולם while MT reads קום "line," a parablepsis or misreading involving one letter.

Psalm 40:6 LXX(H)
לא חפצת [גוף ברית] לי

Psalm 40:6 Sacrifice and offering you did not desire, but **a body you prepared** for me. You have not required burnt offering and sin offering.

Comments: The LXX and Hebrews 10:5 GNT read "a body you prepared" while MT reads "ears you have dug." In a bet-kaph confusion, "prepared" ברית was misread as "dug" כרית and this may have caused a scribe to adjust the word "body" to a word that made a little more sense with "dug," viz. "ears." Alternatively, a defect in the scroll could have made the word "body" illegible resulting in a guess.

Psalm 68:18 Syr(H) cf. Tg
עלית למרום שבית שבי [ותנתן] מתנות [לבני אדם]
ואף סוררים לא ישכנו לפני אלהים:

Psalm 68:18 You have ascended on high. You have led away captives. **And you gave** gifts **to** men; but the rebellious will not dwell in the presence of God.

Comments: The Peshitta Syriac reads ויהבת מוהבתא לבני אנשא which retroverted to Hebrew is= ותנתן מתנות לבני אדם "And you gave gifts to men" cf. Ephesians 4:8 GNT. MT reads לקחת מתנות באדם "You received gifts from men." BHS notes that three of the last four words in the verse are corrupt in MT (=LXX) and suggest the Syriac Peshitta as the best witness. Since the MT also reads slightly different than the Syriac in two other words it would appear that the corruption affected those as well. The pre-Christian Targum also reads with Syriac "you gave."

Psalm 69:22 LXX(H)
לפניהם לפח [ולשלומים] ולמוקש [ומכשול]: תחשכנה

Psalm 69:22 Let their table before them become a snare, **and a retribution**, and a trap, **and a stumbling block**.

Comments: The LXX and Romans 11:9 GNT read "a retribution...a stumbling block" while MT reads "peace" and lacks the last word. The difference in the first word is vocalization, while the last word is lacking from homoioarcton: w-w, or a graphic confusion involving a six letter word beginning with a waw.

Psalm 102:25 LXX(H)
לפנים [יהוה] הארץ יסדת

Psalm 102:25 In the beginning, **LORD**, you established the foundation of the earth. The heavens are the works of your hands.

Comments: The LXX and Hebrews 1:10 GNT have "LORD" while MT lacks the word, possibly from homoioteleuton by sight confusion in a square script: h-m.

Psalm 118:6 LXX(H) Syr
יהוה לִי [בעזרי] לא אירא

Psalm 118:6 The LORD is my **helper**; I will not be afraid. What can man do to me?

Comments: The LXX and Hebrews 13:6 GNT have "helper" while MT lacks the word, from homoioteleuton: y-y.

Proverbs 3:12 LXX(H)

יהוה יוכיח [ויכאב] את [כל] בֵּן [יִרְצֶה]:

Proverbs 3:12 for whom the LORD loves he disciplines, **and punishes every** son he **accepts**.

Comments: The LXX and Hebrews 12:6 GNT read "and punishes every...accepts" while MT reads "and as a father...delights." MT has lost a yod in a misreading of "and punishes" ויכאב as "and as a father" וכאב, and has lost כל "every" from homoioarcton by sight confusion: k-b. Also, MT has vocalized יִרְצֶה "accepts" as יִרְצֶה "delights."

Proverbs 11:31 LXX(H)

הן הצדיק [במאמץ נושע] רשע וחוטא [אָנָה יראה]: אַהב

Proverbs 11:31 Behold, if the righteous is **saved with difficulty, where will** the ungodly and the sinner **appear**?

Comments: The LXX and 1Peter 4:18 GNT read molis sozetai "with difficulty escape/is saved," while MT reads בארץ ישלם "is repaid on earth." Greek sozetai suggests ימלט "escape, deliver" or נושע "saved," the former being the most graphically similar to MT ישלם in the case that the scribe had misread the words, though the latter would seem to fit the context better. The Greek also has pou phanei "where will appear" = אנה יראה which MT has lost from homoioarcton: aleph-aleph.

Isaiah 6:10 LXX(H)

[הָשְׁמַן] לב-העם הזה [ואזניהם] הכבד [ועיניהם השעם] פן-[יראו בעינים ובאזנים ישמעו ולבבם יבינו ושבו ורפאתים]

Isaiah 6:10 For the heart of this people **has** grown dull, and **their** ears sluggish, and have closed **their** eyes, otherwise they might see with **their** eyes, and hear with **their** ears, and understand with **their** heart, and turn back, and **I would** heal **them**.

Comments: In comparison with LXX and Matthew 13:15 GNT, MT has undergone editing from 3rd person plural "their" to 3rd person singular "his."

Isaiah 8:18 LXX(H)
נתן לי [אלהים] לאתות

Isaiah 8:18 Behold, I and the children whom **God** has given me are for signs and wonders in Israel from the LORD of hosts, who dwells in Mount Zion.

Comments: The LXX and Hebrews 2:13 GNT read "God" while MT reads "the LORD." See comments for Genesis 15:6.

Isaiah 10:22-23 LXX(H)
שאר [יושע כי מלה מלאון] וחרוץ שוטף צדקה: 23
כי [מלה] ונחרצה [אדני] עשה בקרב הארץ:

Isaiah 10:22 For though your people, Israel, are as the sand of the sea, a remnant will be **saved**. For he will **fulfill the word and decisively**, overflowing in righteousness. 23 For the **Lord** will carry out **the word** decisively in the midst **of the** earth.

Comments: In comparison with LXX and Romans 9:27-28 GNT these two verses in MT have suffered several misreadings, haplography, a harmonization and an expansion. Verse 21 reads שאר ישוב "remnant return" and when the MT scribe saw ישוב "remnant" followed by a word beginning with a yod he assumed the word was "return" once again. However, according to LXX sothesetai the word actually was "saved" יושע (or, ישגב "set on high/safe." Cf. Proverbs 29:25 LXX).

The word כי "For" was misread as בו "of it" by sight confusion, and מלה "word" was lost from homoioarcton: ml-ml. The next word מלאון "fulfill" was misread as כליון "destruction" by sight confusion in a Paleo-Hebrew script: ml-kl. In the next verse מלה "word" was misread as כלה "destruction," again by sight confusion in a Paleo-Hebrew script: ml-kl. Based on Hebrew Mss and LXX Mss, MT has expanded "Lord" to "Lord, LORD of hosts," possibly as a harmonization to the next verse, and has added "all" before "the earth," a typical scribal expansion well documented.

Isaiah 11:10 LXX(H)
אשר עמד [לנשיא עַל] עַמים אליו

Isaiah 11:10 And in that day there will be a root of Jesse, one who stands up to **rule over** the peoples; to him will the nations seek, and his resting place will be glorious.

Comments: The LXX and Romans 15:12 GNT read archein "rule" = לנשיא lenasi while MT reads לנס lenes "banner," an aural confusion. Also, MT has lost על "over" from homoioarcton: ayin-ayin.

Isaiah 28:16 LXX(H) (sight confusion)
[והמאמין עליו] לא [יבוש]: ושמתי

Isaiah 28:16 Therefore thus says the LORD, "Behold, I am laying in Zion a stone for a foundation, a tried stone, a precious cornerstone of a sure foundation, **and** whoever believes **in him** will not be put to **shame**.

Comments: The LXX and 1Peter 2:6 GNT read ep autw ou me kataischunthe "in him will not be put to shame" = עליו לא יבוש, while MT has lost עליו "in him" from homoioteleuton by sight confusion: yn-yw, and has misread יבוש "shame" as יחיש "hurry," a misreading of two letters in a square script, with yod and waw being among the easiest to confuse.

Isaiah 29:13 LXX(H)
רחק ממני [ותהו] יראתם אתי [מלמדים] מצות אנשים [ומלמדיה]:

Isaiah 29:13 LXX(H) Mss
רחק ממני [ותהו] יראתם אתי [מלמדים] מלמדיה מצות אנשים:

Isaiah 29:13 And the Lord said, "Because these people draw near with their mouth and honor me with their lips, but they have removed their heart far from me, and **in vain** do they worship me, **teaching** the commandments **and instructions** of men.

Comments: The LXX and Matthew 15:9 GNT read maten de "and in vain" = ותהו while MT reads ותהי "and is," a confusion of yod and waw which is easily confused in square script. MT also lacks the word מלמדים "teaching" from homoioarcton: m-m, and reads the final word as singular rather than plural, a possible adjustment after the loss of מלמדים "teaching" from haplography. Alternatively, some LXX Mss have the same word order as Matthew 15:9, which may be the original word order, suggesting a four letter haplography: mlmd-mlmd with subsequent word order rearrangement.

Isaiah 29:14 LXX(H)
ופלא [ואבדתי] חכמת [חכמים] ובינת [נבונים אסתיר]

Isaiah 29:14 Therefore, behold, I will again do a marvelous work among this people, even a marvelous work and a wonder; and **I will** destroy the wisdom of **the wise**, and the discernment of **the** discerning **I will** hide."

In comparison of the LXX, 1 Corinthians 1:19 GNT and MT, the latter has suffered either careless copying or doctrinal edits in at least three places: 1. kai apolo "and I will destroy" = ואבדתי has been changed to ואבדה "and destroyed," 2. ton sopon "the wise" = חכמים has become חכמיו "their wise," 3. suneton "the discerning" = נבונים was changed to נבניו "his discerning ones," and 4. krupso "I will hide" = אסתיר has become תסתתר "will be hidden."

Isaiah 40:5 LXX(H) OL Mss
בשר יחדו [בישע אלהים] כי פי

Isaiah 40:5 The glory of the LORD shall be revealed, and all flesh shall see **the salvation of God** together; for the mouth of the LORD has spoken it."

Comments: The LXX, Old Latin Mss and Luke 3:6 GNT read soterion tou theou "the salvation of God" = בישע אלהים (Cf. Psalm 50:23) while MT lacks the words from homoioarcton by sight confusion: by-ky.

Isaiah 40:8 LXX(H) Mss OL Vg Mss
ציץ ודבר [יהוה] יקום לעולם

Isaiah 40:8 The grass withers, the flower fades; but the word of the **LORD** stands forever."

Comments: LXX(L), OL, Vg Mss and 1Peter 1:25 GNT read "LORD" while MT reads "our God." Cf. comments on Genesis 15:6.

Isaiah 42:4 LXX(H)
בארץ משפט [ולשמו גוים] ייחילו: כה

Isaiah 42:4 He will not grow dim or be crushed, until he has established justice on the earth, and in **his name the nations** will hope."

Comments: The LXX and Matthew 12:21 GNT read "his name the nations" = ולשמו גוים while MT reads ולתרתו איים "his law the coastlands," a misreading in a square script, possibly in reminiscence of 30:9 (law) and 41:5 (coastlands). The letters waw, lamed, waw, yod and mem are in the same positions, and several letters could have been confused in a square script (cf. Habakkuk Pesher), perhaps in a scroll that was damaged in this passage.

Isaiah 52:5 LXX(H)
יהוה תמיד [בגללכם] כל היום שמי מנאץ [בגוים]: לכן

Isaiah 52:5 "Now therefore, what do I do here," says the LORD, "seeing that my people are taken away for nothing? Those who rule over them mock," says the LORD, "and **because of you** my name is continually all the day blasphemed **among the nations**.

Comments: The LXX and Romans 2:24 GNT have "because of you" and "among the nations" while MT lacks the words. The word for "because of you" could have been lost from homoioarcton by sight confusion: b-k, while "among the nations" was apparently lost by a simple omission.

Isaiah 52:15 LXX(H)
לא ספר [עליו] ראו ואשר

Isaiah 52:15 so shall he sprinkle many nations; kings shall shut their mouths at him. For that which was not told about **him**, they will see, and what they have not heard, they will understand.

Comments: The LXX and Romans 15:21 GNT read autou "him" = עליו while MT reads להם "them," from careless copying or unknown editing reason.

Isaiah 53:1 LXX(H)
התבוננו: [יהוה] מי האמין

Isaiah 53:1 LORD, who has believed our message? And to whom has the arm of the LORD been revealed?

Comments: The LXX and John 12:38, etc., GNT have "LORD" while MT lacks the divine name, possibly from a simple omission, or from theological considerations.

Isaiah 53:8 LXX(H) Mss cf. DSS
[בעצרו משפטו] לקח [את] דורו מי ישוחח כי נגזר
מארץ [חייו] מפשע עמי [נֻגַּע למות]

Isaiah 53:8 In his oppression his justice was taken away. Who will consider his generation? For **his life** was cut off from the earth, **led to death** for the transgression of my people.

Comments: LXX and Acts 8:33 GNT read en = בְּ "In," while MT reads מ "From," a bet-mem confusion in a square script. LXX(L) and Acts 8:33 add "his." MT reads lit. "And his generation who will consider" while LXX and GNT lack "And." The latter Mss read zoe autou = חייו "his life" whereas MT transcribed as חיים "living," a waw-mem confusion in Paleo-Hebrew. LXX reads echthe = נֻגַּע "led," while MT has vocalized the same consonantal letters as נֶגַע "the stroke." Lastly, LXX translated as thanaton = למות "death," whereas MT has למו, "to them(?)," having lost a tav in transcription. Cf. P. J. Gentry, JETS 52 (2009), 31-32; DSS 1QIsa(a); LXX(L).

Isaiah 53:9 LXX(H)
עשה ולא־[נמצאה] מרמה בפיו

Isaiah 53:9 And they assigned his grave with the wicked and with the rich in his death; though he had done no wrong, neither was any deceit **found** in his mouth.

Comments: LXX and 1 Peter 2:22 GNT read heurethe = נמצאה "found" while MT lacks the word, from homoioteleuton: h-h.

Isaiah 54:13 LXX(H)
בניך למודי [אלהים] ורב שלום

Isaiah 54:13 All your children shall be taught by **God**; and great shall be the peace of your children.

Comments: The LXX and John 6:45 GNT read "God" while MT reads "the LORD." See comments on Genesis 15:6.

Isaiah 59:20 LXX(H)
[מציון] גואל [וישיב] פשע [מיעקב]

Isaiah 59:20 "A Redeemer will come **from** Zion, and **he** will turn away transgression **from** Jacob," says the LORD.

Comments: In comparison of the LXX, Romans 11:26 GNT and MT, the latter has suffered either careless copying or doctrinal edits in at least three places: 1. ek Sion "from Zion" = מציון has been changed to לציון "to/for Zion," 2. kai apostrepsei "and he will turn away" = וישיב has become ולשבי "and those who turn away," and 3. apo Iakob "from Jacob" = מיעקב was changed to ביעקב "in Jacob."

Isaiah 61:1 LXX(H)
רוח [יהוה] עלי יען [משח אתי] לבשר ענוים שלחני לחבש
לנשברי־לב לקרא לשבוים דרור [ולעורים פקחקוח]:

Isaiah 61:1 The Spirit of the **LORD** is upon me; because **he** has anointed me to preach good news to the poor. He has sent me to bind up the brokenhearted, to proclaim liberty to the captives, and an opening of the eyes to the **blind**;

Comments: The LXX and Luke 4:18 GNT read "LORD" while the MT has expanded the divine name to "Lord GOD," as well as "he" to "LORD." In addition, וְלַעִוְרִים "blind" has been misread as וְלַאֲסוּרִים "bound," possibly in reminiscence of 49:9, and the last word (cf. DSS) has been divided by MT into two words.

Isaiah 65:2 LXX(H)
אל עם [סורר ומרה] ההלכים הדרך

Isaiah 65:2 I have spread out my hands all day long to a disobedient **and obstinate** people, who walk in a way that is not good, following their own thoughts;

Comments: The LXX and Romans 10:21 GNT have "and obstinate" while MT lacks the word, possibly from a simple omission.

Jeremiah 31:12 LXX(H)
בריתי ואנכי [בעלתי] בם נאם־יהוה

Jeremiah 31:32 not according to the covenant that I made with their fathers in the day that I took them by the hand to bring them out of the land of Egypt; which my covenant they broke, and I **disregarded** them," says the LORD.

Comments: The LXX and Hebrews 8:9 GNT understand בעלתי as emelesa "disregarded." The Syriac reads bsjt "despised" while the Arabic cognate ba'ala means "disgusted" (Cf. E. W. Lane, Arabic-English Lexicon 1:228; McDaniel, pp.10-11). MT has misvocalized the word as "a husband."

Hosea 14:2 LXX(H)
ונשלמה [פרי] שפתינו:

Hosea 14:2 Take words with you, and return to the LORD. Tell him, "Forgive all our sins, and accept that which is good, and we will offer the **fruit** of our lips.

Comments: Hebrews 13:15 GNT reads karpon cheileon "the fruit of lips," an allusion to Hosea 14:2 where the LXX has the same two Greek words. MT reads instead "bulls of lips," a misreading of פרי "fruit" as פרים "bulls."

Amos 5:26 LXX(H)
ונשאתם את [סכת מלך] ואת [ריפן] הצלמים כוכב

Amos 5:26 You took up the **tabernacle of Moloch**, the star of your god **Rephan**, your images that you made for yourselves.

Comments: The LXX and Acts 7:43 GNT read "tabernacle of Moloch...Rephan" while MT reads "your king Sikkuth... Kiyyun." Here MT has misread סכת sukkat "tabernacle" as סכות "Sikkut" under the influence of Babylonian culture, since the latter is a Mesopotamian star god, Sakkuth. "Moloch" מֹלֶךְ (Molek) was misinterpreted as melek מֶלֶךְ "king," and was adjusted to the plural מלככם "your king" following the misreading of the previous word sukkat as Sikkut." Lastly, ריפן "Rephan" has been misread in an early square script as כיון "Kiyyun," being once again the name of a Mesopotamian god. The change from Paleo-Hebrew to square script occurred around the time of the Babylonian exile, and in early square script the names appear somewhat similar.

Amos 9:12 LXX(H)
למען [ידרשו] על שארית [אדם] וכל־הגוים

Amos 9:12 that the rest of **mankind** may **seek** after me, and all the nations who are called by my name," says the LORD who does this.

Comments: The LXX and Acts 15:17 GNT read anthropon "mankind" = אדם and ekzetesosin "seek" = ידרשו while MT has misread the words as אדום "Edom" and יירשו "possess."

Habakkuk 1:5 LXX(H)
ראו [בוגדים] והביטו והתמהו תמהו [וָשֹׁמוּ] כִּי [אָנֹכִי] פעל פעל בימיכם

Habakkuk 1:5 "Look, you **scoffers**, and watch, and be utterly amazed, **and perish**; for **I am** working a work in your days which you will not believe though it is told you.

Comments: The LXX and Acts 13:41 GNT read kataphronetai "scoffers" = בוגדים and kai aphanisthete "and perish" = ושמו while MT has misread as בגוים "among the nations," and lacks "and perish" from homoioteleuton: w-w. Also, LXX and GNT ego "I am" appears to have dropped out of MT from homoioteleuton: ky-ky. In the misreading of בוגדים as בגוים a metathesis between waw and gimel is possible.

Habakkuk 2:4 LXX(H)
[עבלה] לא־[שרה] נפשו בו

Habakkuk 2:4 Behold, if he should **draw back** my soul has no **pleasure** in him, but the righteous will live by his faith.

Comments: The LXX and Hebrews 10:38 GNT read huposteiletai "draw back" = עבלה and eudokei "pleasure" = שרה (Cf. Lane 4:1337, 1339; KBS 4:1657; McDaniel, pp.12-14) while MT has misread as עפלה "puff up," a bet-pey confusion, and ישרה "upright" for שרה "pleasure."

Zechariah 13:7 LXX(H) Mss
צבאות [אכה] את הרעה

Zechariah 13:7 "Awake, sword, against my shepherd, and against the man who is close to me," says the LORD of hosts. "**I will** strike the shepherd, and the sheep will be scattered; and I will turn my hand against the little ones.

Comments: LXX manuscripts and Matthew 26:31 GNT read pataxate "I will strike" = akkeh אכה (imperfect 1st sg), while MT has edited to hak הך "Strike" (imperative masc sg).